HERE'S WHAT PEOPLE HAVE SAID ABOUT PHILIP MAFFETONE'S APPROACH TO HEALTH AND FITNESS:

"Dr. Maffetone is a modern-day medicine man whose views, practices, and techniques extend far beyond the turbocharged adrenaline of the exercise kingdom."
—*William R. Katovsky, founding editor of* Inside Triathlon *and* Triathlete *magazines and two-time Ironman*

"The great conductor Arturo Toscanini once remarked, 'Tradition is the last bad performance.' Like Toscanini, Philip Maffetone questions some of the weary tenets of performance training. His stable of athletes is perhaps the purest expression of his craft."
—*John Howard, bicycling legend and coach*

"Dr. Maffetone is one of the most sought-after endurance coaches in the world."   —*Velo News*

ABOUT THE AUTHOR

Dr. Philip Maffetone practiced complementary sports medicine and applied kinesiology for over 20 years. His extensive background in biochemistry and exercise physiology has helped him train many world class and professional athletes, and he has helped many others succeed at general fitness and weight-loss. He also has a doctorate degree in chiropractic and is certified in acupuncture. Among the many athletes he has worked with are running guru George Sheehan, Olympians Priscilla Welch and Lorraine Moller, triathletes Mark Allen and Mike Pigg, and race-car drivers Mario and Michael Andretti. Most importantly, Dr. Maffetone has worked with and helped thousands of people reach their goals of improved health and fitness.

Dr. Maffetone was named *Coach of the Year* in 1994 by *Triathlete* magazine. He served as chairman of the International College of Applied Kinesiology from 1990 to 1994. His recent general audience books include *In Fitness and in Health* and *Training for Endurance; Complementary Sports Medicine*, a textbook, was published in 1999. Dr. Maffetone continues to write and lecture extensively on sports, exercise, diet, and nutrition, and complementary medicine, and his work is seen in many magazines throughout the world. He is currently president of the MAF Group, which publishes the *Maffetone Report*.

The

MAFFETONE
METHOD

The Holistic, Low-Stress,

No-Pain Way to

Exceptional Fitness

DR. PHILIP
MAFFETONE

Ragged Mountain Press / McGraw-Hill

Camden, Maine • New York • San Francisco • Washington, D.C. • Auckland
Bogotá • Caracas • Lisbon • London • Madrid • Mexico City • Milan
Montreal • New Delhi • San Juan • Singapore • Sydney • Tokyo • Toronto

Ragged Mountain Press

A Division of The McGraw-Hill Companies

10 9 8 7 6 5 4 3 2 1

Copyright © 2000 Philip Maffetone

All rights reserved. The publisher takes no responsibility for the use of any of the materials or methods described in this book, nor for the products thereof. The name "Ragged Mountain Press" and the Ragged Mountain Press logo are trademarks of The McGraw-Hill Companies. Printed in the United States of America.

Library of Congress Cataloging-in-Publication Data
Maffetone, Philip
        The Maffetone method : the holistic, low-stress, no-pain way to exceptional fitness / Philip Maffetone.
        p.   cm.
        Includes bibliographical references and index.
        ISBN 0-07-134331-8
        1. Physical fitness.   2. Exercise.   I. Title.
RA781.M335   1999
613.7'1—dc21   99-22495
                                                    CIP

Questions regarding the content of this book should be addressed to
Ragged Mountain Press
P.O. Box 220
Camden, ME 04843
www.raggedmountainpress.com

Questions regarding the ordering of this book should be addressed to
The McGraw-Hill Companies
Customer Service Department
P.O. Box 547
Blacklick, OH 43004
Retail customers: 1-800-262-4729
Bookstores: 1-800-722-4726

This book is printed on 55-lb Lakeside.

Printed by R.R. Donnelley & Sons, Crawfordsville, IN
Design by Susan Newman and Dan Kirchoff
Production by Dan Kirchoff
Edited by Tom McCarthy, Joanne Allen, and D. A. Oliver

Ativan, Elavil, Prozac, Tofranil, and Valium are registered trademarks.

The information in *The Maffetone Method* is based on the author's practice and professional experiences and is not intended to replace medical advice. It is not the author's intent to diagnose or prescribe. Before beginning any program, consult with your physician, and address any specific concerns with your physician.

Case studies in this book are from actual experiences, although names have been changed to protect clients' privacy.

DEDICATION
To all those who seek improved health and fitness through a better understanding of his and her own body and mind.

CONTENTS

FOREWORD

Peak performance fitness and lifestyle fitness are separated only by volume. Someone interested in improving his or her overall health and quality of life through exercise can use the same principles an elite healthy athlete uses to win a race like the Ironman. The big difference between training to win the Ironman and training for life is the distance—the principles are the same! I used Phil's workout structure during my competitive years and was able to win the Ironman six times. And I still use Phil's training principles to keep me fit *for life.*

There are several reasons I feel Dr. Maffetone's principles are so powerful and effective. First and foremost, they are easy to follow. Like everyone else, I have constraints on my time and on mental energy available for training. If a program is so complicated that I spend most of my time trying to figure it out, it will fail for me. Phil's approach avoids this major pitfall so common with a lot of other schedules.

Phil had based his program on the real world, another reason for the success of his methods. Many coaches base their recommendations on research done in a lab under specific and controlled conditions. More often than not, the results from this research miss the mark in the real world. I know Phil's program and principles work because I've tested them for over a decade in the real world of elite athletics. And I continue to use these principles to enhance my quality of life through a balanced athletic training schedule that helps improve my health and reduce the level of stress in my life.

If you have ever left a program by the wayside—and even if you think the program you're using is "the one"—check out the Maffetone Method. I think you will find this method easy to follow and one that will get you the results you are after!

Mark Allen
6-Time Ironman World Champion

PREFACE

I was first taught about exercise, including its benefits and how-tos, in a very traditional way—both through experience and from my studies. This included my years of high school and college sports, when I became a highly ranked track and field athlete. In college, courses in anatomy, physiology, and biomechanics led to more studies, including courses in exercise physiology. These academic experiences included cookbook prescriptions, the "no pain, no gain" approach, and many other teachings by professors and coaches that at the time seemed to make sense. However, once I was in private practice, applying these principles in real life often resulted in more disappointment than success. I was so convinced of the truth of these exercise myths that when they failed to work, I presumed that it was somehow the patient's fault, for not being disciplined, not working hard enough, or simply not being truthful.

Fortunately, I quickly realized that the fault was my own. Early on, it became clear that I was a double victim of the "no pain, no gain" approach: I had been taught it, and now I was passing it on to others. This approach was not only less effective in the long run but unhealthy. Measuring the patient's progress—or lack thereof—forced me to rethink my approach. I realized that the human body would progress athletically naturally if it was not overstressed. I decided to see how successful an average person could be by following a no-pain approach to exercise. I was embarrassed that I had subscribed to the "no pain, no gain" theory, so well entrenched in our society.

My new method was almost too easy! And surprisingly, this healthy approach to exercise worked not only for the average person but also for competitive athletes, who improved their personal-best performances and finished in first place in local races. Some went on to even higher levels; some even achieved world-class status, winning national and world championship events.

In addition to a better exercise model, I developed a more successful approach to diet and nutrition that was also very different from the current dogma.

These "cutting-edge" methods made me different from most of my peers, and I was told that my practice would never grow and be successful. But what I found was that patients who were not getting answers, relief, or success began coming to me as a last resort. Within a few short years new patients had to wait weeks and then months for an appointment. Word of mouth was promoting my practice to great heights.

I was also intrigued about how people were motivated. It became relatively easy to work with a person one-on-one, but I felt the need to promote my hard-learned lessons to larger audiences. Eventually I began to deliver my advice in front of groups of people and to write articles. I wanted to get across the important idea that people had to take more responsibility for their own health and fitness rather than rely on me, another professional, or our ailing health care system. This led me to develop a clear philosophy with numerous approaches, tests, and other items described in this book.

As the years passed, this method passed the test of time. It has been clinically proven, not only by me but by other professionals who employ it with their clients and patients. And as the bibliography shows, there is a scientific basis for this approach. Although it is rewarding to see people achieve great feats in sports, it is even more rewarding to see the average person, the one just trying to get healthier and more fit, achieve the great benefits that come from an improved quality of life.

INTRODUCTION

If you are reading this, you've taken the first step toward improving your health and fitness. Your starting point doesn't matter. Whether you've never exercised in your life or are looking for a competitive edge in your next race; whether you're overweight, recovering from a serious medical problem, or working through a nagging sports injury, the improvement you seek is feasible, and getting there can be half the fun.

The Maffetone Method stresses simplicity and common sense. Once you learn a few commonly misunderstood concepts of exercise and diet, you'll be well on your way. The most inexpensive and perhaps most successful workout device is the one you possess naturally: no machine will do more for you than you can do with your own body. Dramatic benefits from exercise can be attained by easy walking for 30 minutes, five days a week. To do more, such as running a marathon, will require additional training, but never to the point of pain. And you don't need expensive shoes, which studies have shown actually promote injury.

But exercise in and of itself is not the guaranteed pathway to health. In fact, one of the first things you'll learn is that it's possible to be fit yet still unhealthy—a description that applies to many world-class athletes. The Maffetone Method is neither a complicated program nor a strenuous one. It does not lead participants to dream of the day it will end. Once you understand the concepts behind it, you'll see that the Maffetone Method is a program you can stick with for life—and what's more, you'll *want* to. And it's a program that builds on itself. The longer you participate, the more you'll understand about yourself, and the better you'll be able to customize it to fit *your* needs, not someone else's.

In various forms, the Maffetone Method has worked for nonathletes who were overweight, exhausted, and depressed; for triathlete champions Mark Allen and Mike Pigg; for ultramarathoner Stu Mittleman; for Olympians Lorraine Moller and Priscilla Welch; and for thousands of athletes and beginners around the world. It will show anyone, including someone recovering from a heart attack or suffering from conditions such as high blood pressure, high cholesterol, diabetes, or obesity, how to reclaim his or her life.

The Maffetone Method takes a holistic approach to finding the right program for you. It will allow you to define your goal, whether it be losing the spare tire that now strains the buttons on your trousers, walking up a flight of stairs without pausing to catch your breath, running around the block, or finishing a marathon. The Maffetone Method will help you to set guidelines not just for what kind of exercise you do but for what you eat and how you react to stress. Consider this: While millions of people seek to reduce stress with regular exercise, many ultimately *add* stress to their lives by exercising too rigorously. Rest is important to any exercise program. When planning rest days (and easy ones), consider your work stress too. For example, if Monday is always your busiest or hardest day on the job, you probably shouldn't train that day.

The Maffetone Method eschews canned exercise prescriptions. In this book you won't be advised to do something like "Run a mile four times a week, do 200 pushups, then jump rope for an hour." Such general advice ignores too much of what is unique to you and your daily life. It's not unlike the old proverb "Give me a fish and you feed me today. Teach me to fish and you feed me for a lifetime." The Maffetone Method will teach you to fish.

The Maffetone Method will give you unlimited energy, make you burn more body fat, and improve the quality of your life—forever. It is based on a number of scientifically proven concepts known to few people other than exercise professionals. "No pain, no gain," while an intriguing advertising message and a temporarily effective exhortation from a high school varsity coach, is quite simply wrong. When you exercise strenuously, your body is programmed to burn *less* fat. To encourage your body to burn *more* fat all day long, you must keep your heart rate within certain target levels, the formula for which is simple. In fact, when you finish a workout, you should actually feel as if you could easily do it again.

Here's a brief overview of other important features of the Maffetone Method:

▶ The best exercise for burning fat and improving your health is aerobic, which can take the form of walking, swimming, cycling, running, dancing, rowing, skating, cross-country skiing, or some other activity you can do for an extended period.

▶ Exercise should be fun. If it's a chore, something's not right. Your workouts are too long, their intensity is too high, or you don't have the right training partner.

▶ Excess stress is bad. Now, this is not a surprising statement, but consider how insidious stress can be. Excessive stress is one of the top causes of increased body fat! It can lead to low energy, insomnia, and a diminished sexual drive, among other things. Not only that, but an improper exercise program can increase stress, and a stressful day at the office prompts the same physiological response as an improper workout.

▶ Many people eat far more carbohydrates than necessary. And more people than we realize are carbohydrate intolerant, a condition that can lead to excess body fat, depression, intestinal bloating, excessive sleepiness, and addictions to sweets and caffeine.

▶ Certain dietary fats are good.

Part 1 of this book discusses in far greater detail the basic concepts of the Maffetone Method. It is important to understand these basics before moving on. Part 2, starting with chapter 11, tells you how to begin, modify, and expand your program.

The Maffetone Method Questionnaire

Before we move on, take a few minutes to answer the following questions. Your answers will constitute the first step in analyzing where you are in the health-and-fitness continuum and deciding where to go from there.

1. Do you often find yourself tired, especially in the after noon?

2. Do you get dizzy when you stand too quickly?

3. Are your eyes sensitive to light, or do you have difficulty driving at night?

4. Do you have asthma or allergies?

5. Do you experience muscle or joint discomfort in your lower back, knees, or ankles?

6. Have you ever experienced a mood shift after the season changed?

7. Do you have trouble sleeping?

8. Do you sometimes feel depressed?

9. Has your sex drive decreased?

10. Do you tire quickly?

11. Do you get sleepy after eating?

12. Have you frequently experienced intestinal bloating after meals?

13. Do you find yourself often craving sweets or caffeine?

14. Does your family have a history of diabetes, heart disease, or stroke?

15. Have you noticed a recent weight gain?

16. *Has it become harder for you to lose weight?*

17. *Do you smoke, drink coffee daily, or both?*

18. *Do you have borderline high blood pressure?*

19. *Are your cholesterol or triglyceride levels high?*

20. *Do you experience a shortness of breath after walking up a flight of stairs?*

21. *Do you frequently experience unexplained aches and pains?*

22. *Have you had more than one cold in the last six months?*

23. *Have you moved your belt out a notch in the last six months?*

24. *Have you found you can't walk as far as you did a year ago?*

25. *Do you sometimes experience numbness or cold hands and feet?*

26. *Given the chance, do you drive or take a cab rather than walk?*

27. *Are you frequently thirsty?*

The Key

Questions 1 to 9 deal with symptoms of excess stress. If you answered "yes" to three or more, see chapter 2.

Questions 10 to 19 deal with carbohydrate intolerance. If you answered "yes" to three or more, see chapters 9 and 20.

Questions 20 to 27 deal with aerobic deficiency. If you answered "yes" to three or more, see the sidebar on pages 10 and 11 and see chapters 9 and 10.

The Method

> The Maffetone Method is a cycle of health and renewal: Assess yourself, set goals, then select plans to reduce stress, build your aerobic base, and improve your diet. Begin your program, continually monitoring your progress. When you've reached your first set of goals, return to the starting point and begin again. Each of these steps is explained in much greater detail later, but this will give you an idea of where you're going.

1. **Assess**

- *Where are you? Fitness to any degree requires reducing excessive stress, building your aerobic base, and eliminating poor dietary habits. Answer the questionnaire on pages 4 and 5 to find out where you stand.*
- *Where are you going? Before embarking on an exercise program, know what you want. Set a main focus: this may be somewhat general, such as to get into good shape, losing weight and body fat, or to compete in a race. Make your goals realistic, but don't be afraid to dream. Secondary goals are also important, and come with the same rules. These may include attaining a certain weight or clothing size, being able to maintain a workout schedule without injury, or reducing your blood pressure.*

2. **Select**

- *Choose a plan to reduce stress: identify the sources of stress in your life (remember, one could be too much exercise), and eliminate those you can and reduce the ones you can't (for some options, see chapter 2).*

The Maffetone Method

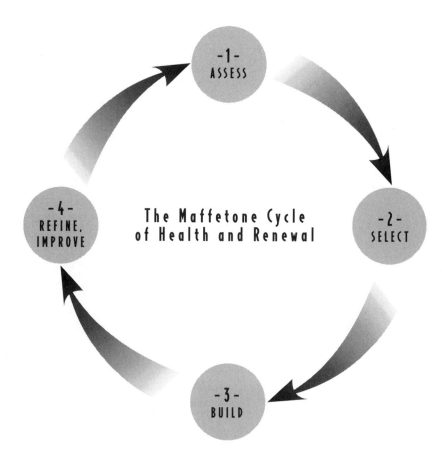

The Maffetone Cycle
of Health and Renewal

-1-
ASSESS

-2-
SELECT

-3-
BUILD

-4-
REFINE,
IMPROVE

- *Choose an aerobic fat-burning method. Reject "No Pain, No Gain." There's a big difference between "health" and "fitness." You can be fit without being healthy. Exercise should reduce stress, not increase it.*
- *Exercise is necessary to help regulate your body's fat-burning mechanisms, and there is a simple test to see if you're too fat. All you need is a tape measure. See below, then go aerobic. (See chapter 4.)*
- *Choose a diet. Aerobic exercise promotes stress reduction and fat burning, but without proper nutrition you'll never achieve the best results (see chapter 20). Take the two-week carbohydrate test. Learn the good, bad, and ugly dietary fats.*

- *Choose your exercise "equipment." Studies have clearly shown that most modern exercise shoes, especially the expensive ones or the overprotective types, can cause injury. Indeed, a strong argument can be made for exercising barefoot when conditions permit. At other times, finding the right shoes necessary for protection isn't hard. In fact, it's a lot less complicated than choosing from among the overly expensive, inappropriate shoes that dominate store shelves. (See chapter 15.)*
- *Choose your anaerobic component (optional). Knowing whether to add anaerobic work to your program is the key to making the anaerobic component work for rather than against you.*

3. Build
- *Develop your aerobic base: set a target heart rate. Whether you walk, run, swim, bike, dance, row, or cross-country ski, the first thing you must do is set a target heart rate to hit the "fat-burning zone" (see chapter 6).*
- *Measure your progress. The Maximum Aerobic Function test (chapter 7) is a simple way to tell you precisely how your aerobic conditioning is improving— and whether it's time to slow down.*

Is Your Workout Working?

Here are some questions that may help you decide whether your workout plan is working for you or against you:

1. *Have you been able to measure your exercise progress?*
2. *Is your energy good from the time you wake up until you go to bed?*
3. *Are you free from injuries, even seemingly minor aches and pains?*
4. *Is your body fat at a controllable level?*
5. *Do you look forward to working out (i.e., is it fun)?*
6. *Do you feel good after your workout?*

If you cannot answer "yes" to all these questions, you may need to modify your program.

4. **Refine and Improve**

Is your program really giving you what you want? (See Is Your Workout Working, left.) Review and focus on your primary and secondary goals on a regular basis.

5. **When You Reach Your Goals, Return to Step 1, Reassess, and Start Again**

Common sense, low intensity, self directed: The Maffetone Method will work for anyone interested in improved fitness, both mental and physical. To allow the program to work, you must address stress, aerobic function, and diet. As with putting new tires on a rough-running car with dirty spark plugs, working to improve only one of those components fails to recognize the relationship and influence of the others. And as you make inroads into increasing your aerobic base, reducing your stress, and improving your diet, the path to total fitness becomes smoother—and your knowledge of yourself will become deeper.

Too Fat?

A tape measure, a few seconds, and a brief calculation are all you need to get a reasonably accurate gauge of whether you are too fat.

1. Measure your waist circumference (inches or centimeters) at belly-button level.
2. Measure your hip circumference at its widest part.
3. Divide the waist measurement by the hip measurement.

A ratio above 0.9 in men and 0.8 in women may indicate that a significant proportion of body fat comes from excess carbohydrates in the diet, especially the refined type found in bagels and all sugars. This is not good; see chapters 4 and 20 to find out why.

Are You Aerobically Deficient?

Answering "yes" to three or more of questions 20 to 27 on page 5 may point to the fact that you are aerobically deficient—which means your aerobic muscles, including their fat-burning capability, are not functioning optimally. Here's why this is important:

1. **Fatigue.** *This may be the most common complaint of the average person. It may be fatigue in the morning (difficulty getting out of bed), in the afternoon (a very low period in the mid-afternoon), or all day. It may be physical fatigue or mental fatigue, the latter impairing your concentration and your ability to focus on your work. In extreme cases exhaustion is the word that best describes the feeling. Fatigue, or sleepiness, following meals may be related to excess carbohydrates in your diet (see chapter 20).*

2. **Blood sugar stress.** *This problem is more difficult to evaluate without blood tests, but the symptoms include frequent hunger, feeling shaky if meals are delayed or missed, and cravings for sweets or caffeine. This problem is often associated with a carbohydrate intolerance, the inability to eat a high-carbohydrate diet without excess fat storage, and the accompanying blood sugar stress. Most individuals with this problem are following a diet high in carbohydrates and low in fats (see chapters 9 and 20).*

3. **Increased body fat.** *Some people eat a diet that has the right number of calories and is not too high in fats, and they exercise regularly but still gain weight and body fat. This stored body fat can find its way to any area: hips, abdomen, arms, even the arteries. Where the body stores it may be mostly a consequence of genetics, and you can't "spot" reduce. More upper-body fat (especially in the abdomen) may indicate that you're eating a diet that is too high in carbohydrates, much of which turns to fat and is stored; bread, sweets, cereals, potatoes, and other carbohydrates may be more of a problem than dietary fat (see chapter 20).*

4. **Structural injuries.** *Joint injuries are common and may be due to the lack of aerobic muscle support around your joints. The lower back, knee, ankle, and foot are most vulnerable to structural injury as a result of aerobic deficiency syndrome (ADS). These problems may be chronic; sometimes the injury recurs at the same site, and other times it seems to "travel" from one area to another. This often prevents regular exercise, creating a vicious cycle. Many of these physical problems can resolve themselves if you can break the*

cycle: find a workout that won't aggravate your injury, such as swimming, cycling, or water aerobics. Remember, it doesn't take much effort to build a good aerobic system (see chapters 4 and 9).

5. **Menstrual and menopausal symptoms.** These two common problems in women are often associated with ADS and with an imbalance in adrenal hormones—specifically, high levels of cortisol and low levels of DHEA (dehydroepiandosterone, an adrenal hormone). In addition, amenorrhea (the cessation of the menstrual period) is often associated with excessive exercising and overtraining (see chapter 10).

6. **Reduced endurance.** This is most evident in an inability to continue to perform well all day long. For the competitive athlete, longer workouts become more difficult and competitive skills lessen. And the Maximum Aerobic Function (MAF) test, perhaps one of the best methods of evaluating aerobic function, shows a decline in performance (see chapters 4 and 7).

7. **Mental and emotional stress.** Common symptoms include feelings of depression, anxiety, or a clinical depression. This problem may come and go, perhaps appearing only at certain times of the month, or it may be constant (see chapters 3, 9, and 10).

8. **Insomnia.** In the type of sleep disturbance associated with ADS, it's easy to fall asleep (often because you're so tired), but then you wake in the middle of the night and have a difficult time getting back to sleep. You're seemingly full of energy and wonder why you lack energy during the day. Many people say the need to urinate awakens them, but more often you wake first, and the need to go to the bathroom is secondary (see chapter 2).

9. **Poor circulation.** Because there is so much circulation in aerobic muscle fibers, poor aerobic capacity usually results in a lesser number of functional blood vessels. This reduces the amount of circulation. The classic symptoms include cold hands and feet and sometimes being cold all over. Varicose veins and hemorrhoids may also accompany this problem.

10. **Sexual dysfunction.** The most common sexual dysfunction is a reduced sex drive. It's normal to have a desire for sex throughout your life, not just when you're in your twenties. When you're aerobically deficient, you're too tired in the evening and the hormones (those that fuel the desire for sex, such as testosterone) are low. Sexual dysfunction is a frequent cause of stress, which then further aggravates the problem (see chapters 2 and 9).

Part 1

UNDERSTANDING THE BASICS

1

Defining Exercise

> The medical literature is full of studies showing the benefits of working out. But rarely are we told how to do it right. And the media doesn't help—with images of fast-paced aerobic dance classes, marathoners sprinting to the finish and collapsing, and of course all those pictures that portray "the agony of defeat."

Proper exercise has two primary components. One is that it's done in a balanced way; in particular this means that it should comprise a balance between aerobic and anaerobic exercise and the right training equation. This is the educated approach. When this path is taken, you can obtain the full benefits of exercise, including increased fat burning and energy and many others discussed in this book. The other primary component is fun. This is a very simple and straightforward concept. Working out is fun when it is properly done. Throughout this book I discuss a variety of components of a fitness program that can reduce or eliminate the fun of exercise when they are not done right. This applies especially to balance.

In a sense, this is a book on the educational aspects of exercise. It should also inspire you, clear up the many myths you encounter, and help you modify, fine-tune, or start a program based on your needs. Unfortunately, most people get caught up in a guessing game when it comes to working out. If you're going to guess, you're most likely going to get in trouble, in which case you might actually be better off as a couch potato. In short, don't just do it, do it right.

Before taking the first step, or improving your current program, you should understand some very important exercise concepts. Not only will they help you understand exercise better but they can help you avoid the common regression periods that most exercisers encounter. In addition, if you can define the various components of exercise, you'll be able to ignore the commercials for ab machines, the lure of overtraining, and the "no pain, no gain" myth, whether from trainers, exercise partners, or family members. In short, once you understand the big picture, you'll accomplish your goals and have fun doing it.

A main focus of this book is balance. Therefore, concepts are often paired. Like the Chinese concept of opposites—yin and yang— these paired concepts help set the stage for a more complete understanding. If we don't have balance, we create imbalance, which can lead to various physical, chemical, and mental signs and symptoms called injuries.

There's no better teaching tool than experience. We all have experiences, and ideally we learn from them. One of my more profound experiences was getting back into shape after a long period of stress and illness. I was nearing the end of my school years and ready to enter private practice. But physical illness due to stress had sidelined me. I was not just inactive and run down: on several occasions I had to be hospitalized.

As part of the recovery process I decided to begin walking. At first, even when I ascended a short flight of stairs I had to stop halfway to rest. A 10-minute walk was my limit. But soon I was walking 20, 25, and then 30 minutes. As I started to feel better, my walk became a bit more brisk, and a year later I was walking 45 minutes to an hour five days a week.

One day, following my walk, I watched the Boston Marathon on TV. "These people are really healthy, if they can run 26 miles," I thought. After more than two years of walking, I wondered how healthy I really was, and I thought that perhaps I should "test" myself. I thought the New York City Marathon, at the end of the year, would be a good test of my health. I was a great runner in high school and in college, and it would be good to run again. So I began walking faster, gradually working some jogging into my workouts, and eventually I began to run longer. All this training led to my marathon test.

The cannon that announced the start of the marathon was so loud that it shook the Verrazano Bridge. The crowd of 18,000 runners began to move. All went well through the first 10 miles. Though the excitement made me run a bit quicker than I had planned, I felt great. By 15 miles I felt as I had expected: tired but able to continue. Within the next couple of miles, however, I began to shiver. Even though I had been drinking plenty of water, I was dehydrated. And I was craving cotton candy. How odd that seemed.

After about 18 miles I no longer could feel my feet. I stopped to have a look: they were numb but still there. That was when I began talking to myself. "My hamstrings are cramping," I said out loud. At the same time, I realized that I wasn't thinking rationally. All I could remember was my goal: to finish the race, proving that I was healthy.

Apparently I looked worse than I felt, for two officials tried to take me off the course, but I wouldn't stop. Somehow I fought my way through the next few miles. I knew the end was near because I was in Central Park—a discovery I made when I ran into a TV camera in the middle of the road. As the pain became more intense, the crowds got louder, and for the first time in quite a while I had a clear view. I could see the finish line. I have very little memory of those last few miles, but I'll always remember the finale.

Someone hung a medal around my neck, my reward for finishing, and what little fluid was in me came out as tears. I recall thinking that I had passed the test: I had proved that I was healthy. But something wasn't right.

The next thing I knew, I was in the first-aid tent near the finish line. Lying on the dozens of cots in the tent were finishers who were clearly in pain and who were being treated by doctors, nurses, and EMTs. But proud finishers they were. Looking around I asked myself, "Are these people really healthy?" I knew then that I hadn't really proved my health. But I had learned an important lesson, one that would benefit not only me but also those I would work with for decades to come: I had made myself fit enough to run 26.2 miles, but this fitness was different from health. From that point on, I thought about my new goal. I would improve my health and balance it with fitness.

Health and Fitness

Two words tossed around as casually as a pair of running shoes are *health* and *fitness*. But the difference between them forms the foundation of an exercise philosophy and a workout ethic.

Health is a state in which all the body's parts, including the muscles, nerves, bones, hormones, organs, and glands, are in balance, or what some call "harmony." A perfect state of health may not be attainable, but always improving our health is something we can all strive for.

Unfortunately, many people assume that health necessarily declines with age. While it is common for health to decline with age, the decline need not be significant. The more we care for our body, the healthier it will become and the longer we will be able to withstand the adverse effects of aging. We have the potential to increase our brain power as we age, get into great physical shape, perhaps the best shape of our lives, and to feel better than ever. This is one of the benefits of proper exercise.

Fitness is the ability to be physically active. For some, this means working out; for others, it means playing tennis again after years of disability; and for some it means being a Master's athlete. If you work out four times a week, you're probably more fit than the person who doesn't exercise. If you win your club's tennis tournament, you're the fittest tennis player there.

But your fitness does not necessarily reflect your health. And being healthy won't necessarily make you a fit athlete. Health and fitness are two different things. What's important is to balance the two, to become both as healthy and as fit as possible considering your potential, schedule, and desires.

A common imbalance in industrialized societies exists in the person who is fit but unhealthy. The majority of athletes—the thousands I've seen in practice—fit this description. They strive to get into better and better shape through training, but often at the expense of their health. Take, for example, the injuries. With few exceptions, an injury is due to a decline in the health of the person who's injured. (Exceptions include major trauma, such as from a fall from a bike or a collision with another player.)

Most injuries arise from a long-standing imbalance in a person's health, such as a muscular imbalance (which can cause an injury to the bone, joint, or muscle), a nutritional problem (e.g., a calcium deficiency, which can in turn result in weak bones, which can lead to a stress fracture), or a nervous-system stress caused by improper exercise shoes (resulting in a knee problem).

Some individuals are willing to sacrifice their health in order to achieve more fitness, such as by taking performance-enhancing drugs. But more common are those who want to lose weight or get into shape in an unreasonably short time. These people may exercise excessively, causing an injury. This scenario is common in January, after many people abuse themselves over the holidays, and again in the spring, when they want to be sure they will be able to fit into their summer clothes. Others suddenly decide to get into shape fast. This often occurs after seeing an infomercial for some new exercise gadget or reading about a special rate at the local gym or in anticipation of an upcoming fortieth birthday. Attempting to make up for lost time is another way to develop an imbalance between health and fitness.

> **Health** A state in which all the body's parts, including the muscles, nerves, bones, hormones, organs, and glands, are in balance.
> **Fitness** The ability to be physically active.

Aerobic and Anaerobic

Both *aerobic* and *anaerobic* refer to specific systems in the body, much like the many other systems you may be more familiar with, such as the digestive, skeletal, and muscular systems.

Ask most exercisers what the word *aerobic* means, and you'll hear words like *breathing* and *oxygen*. These definitions came out of academic circles, especially in relation to microbes (some need oxygen to survive, others are destroyed by oxygen). There are also complex processes in the body that can be labeled aerobic and anaerobic. But humans are not microbes, and our whole body requires oxygen to live, so I choose not to use the definition of aerobic associated with oxygen or breathing.

A more important and practical distinction of aerobic function is that it is related to the use of body fat for energy. All muscles need energy to work—to carry us through the day and especially through a workout. Although aerobic muscles also burn sugar (glucose) for energy, these muscles can also burn significant amounts of body fat for energy.

Not only can the aerobic muscles burn fat but they are well endowed with blood vessels and have many other benefits (see chapter 4). Aerobic muscle fibers are sometimes referred to as "red" because of the numerous blood vessels they contain and because of the presence of myoglobin, a pigment containing iron. Throughout this book I often refer to the more efficient fat-burning mechanism and other important benefits of proper aerobic exercise.

Unfortunately, if your body's aerobic system is not well developed, you won't be able to burn much fat. Not only will you store this substance (on your hips, thighs, and maybe even in your blood vessels) but you'll have to rely on the anaerobic system to provide you with energy.

DIFFERENTIATING AEROBIC AND ANAEROBIC FUNCTION

MUSCLE FIBER TYPE	AEROBIC	ANAEROBIC
Predominant energy from	fat	sugar
Energy	long term (endurance)	short term (sprinting)
Blood vessels	many	few
Physical activity	long duration	very short duration

The fat-burning capability of the aerobic system truly sets it apart from the body's anaerobic function, which is associated with sugar burning. *Anaerobic* muscle fibers don't burn fat. They get their

The Maffetone Method

Muscle Fibers

Aerobic and anaerobic muscle fibers are organized differently in various animals. In chickens and other birds, for example, whole muscles contain either aerobic or anaerobic fibers. This pattern can be seen in a cooked chicken. The dark meat is the aerobic muscle, containing pigment from blood vessels, and is more fatty (and therefore tastier). The white meat is drier (less fat) and has no red pigments. Human muscle fibers are not arranged in the same way. All human skeletal muscles (as opposed to the "smooth muscles" found in the blood vessels and intestines) contain a mix of both aerobic and anaerobic fibers; the vast majority, however, are aerobic.

energy from glycogen, a form of sugar stored in muscles and the liver, and from blood sugar. These reserves are relatively scarce compared with fat stores (even in lean individuals), supplying energy only for a short period of time. If we relied only on these sources of energy, we'd have only a few minutes worth of energy and then we'd be exhausted. This is the system used in sprinting, whether on the track or when running for the bus. More important, it's also the system that is stimulated when you're under stress. And worse, too much anaerobic stimulation, from exercise or stress, can impair aerobic function. (The important relationship between exercise and stress is discussed in chapter 2.)

It's important to note that measuring the body's capacity to burn fat is relatively easy (although not always convenient). You can determine the amount of fat and sugar your body uses with a gas analyzer, which measures the carbon dioxide you breathe out and the oxygen you take in. For example, while riding a stationary bike, walking or running on a treadmill, or even at rest, you breathe into a tube, where your carbon dioxide and oxygen are collected. The amount of carbon dioxide and oxygen collected can be used to determine the amount and percentage of fat and sugar burned at specific levels of intensity, measured by heart rate. For example, during easy exercise your body may obtain 90 percent of its energy from sugar and only 10 percent from fat. This might indicate that your aerobic system is not functioning as efficiently as it might.

Proper exercise over a three-month period could result in improvements to your aerobic system; for example, your body might get 50 percent of its energy from sugar and 50 percent from fat. With more aerobic improvements, you might burn even more fat for energy during exercise, which also means you'll burn more fat even when you're sleeping!

Aerobic   The ability to obtain more energy through increased fat burning.

Anaerobic   The increased use of sugar for energy, and diminished fat burning.

Activity and Exercise

Many people place *exercise* in a neat little box; they treat it as a separate routine to be set aside for certain days. But exercise can be defined as purposeful activity, usually done separate and apart from the normal daily chores. In a real sense, it provides us with physical movement no longer provided for in the course of a normal day. You could say that exercise is an artificial way to induce *activity*.

Consider that the human body has evolved with very high levels of natural physical activity as a primary function. Physical activity has helped us to protect ourselves, to secure food, and to shelter ourselves for millions of years. Unfortunately, only in the past few decades have humans dramatically reduced their natural level of physical activity. Enter exercise.

Exercise becomes the separate habit most of us need to employ just to maintain a level of physical activity closer to normal. In a sense, exercise is artificial activity. Better to do that than risk falling into a "deficiency" of exercise, resulting in the aerobic deficiency syndrome (see chapter 9).

As our population ages, fewer of us remember the high levels of natural activity performed by our parents or grandparents. A typical day was a very active one, beginning with morning chores, including making breakfast, bringing in wood for the fire, feeding the animals, or other activities. Some of us still perform these tasks today, but most of us take the elevator to the first floor at work, spend extra time finding a parking place close to the front door of the store, and use the microwave or the food processor to whip up some fast food or get takeouts. Through exercise we can make up for the potential deficiencies created by living in a modern industrialized society.

In addition to finding time for a short period of artificial activity, whether it's a walk, an aerobics class, or time in front of the TV on a stationary bike, we can make a few changes in our daily life that will bring back some of our lost natural activity. Here are some ideas:

▶ *When going shopping, park farther from, instead of closer to, the store. This will give your body some more walking to and from the store. It may also keep those annoying dents off your car.*

▶ *If you're going up or down a flight or two in your office building, apartment, or hotel, take the stairs. For most people, even walking three or four flights down is not taxing.*

▶ *If you take the subway to work, get off a station before or after your normal stop and walk a few extra blocks. It can serve as a time for meditation before work and mental recovery after.*

▶ *At lunchtime, take the long way to the cafeteria. The extra distance can provide a time to relax, which can be good for digestion. A slow stroll back to work would be great too.*

▶ *When waiting for the bus, airplane, train, or people you're meeting, don't just stand there: walk back and forth. So what if others think you're pacing. They may eventually follow suit.*

Of course, added activity and exercise take time. You have the time; you just have to make the added activity and exercise a priority in your life. Your health and fitness will benefit greatly. In addition, your work performance, whether you're an executive, a student, or a homemaker, might also improve significantly.

> ***Activity*** The natural physical activity that is part of everyday chores.
>
> ***Exercise*** A separate activity, purposefully performed; artificial activity.

Training and Endurance

Training encompasses the whole program of exercise, as organized or fragmented, and even absent, as it may be. Training incorporates your workout. Unfortunately, most people do not extend the definition to include the other important aspect of training: rest and recovery. Without sufficient recovery from your workout, you may overextend yourself, resulting in overtraining.

It may be best to define training as an equation:

training = workout + rest

Through proper training, mixed with sufficient rest to recover so that your next workout session is not stressful, you can increase aerobic fitness and thus your endurance.

Endurance is the development of sufficient aerobic fitness benefits to perform with improved efficiency over longer periods of time. In short, endurance is an aerobic quality. Endurance is easy to see in competitive athletes. As effective training proceeds, the athlete can run longer distances without tiring, eventually covering more distance in less time. In order to do this, the body must shift its energy to burn more fat since fat provides much more potential energy for endurance.

Competitive athletes are not the only ones who need endurance. Executives, laborers, homemakers, students, professionals—everyone who works physically and mentally—requires endurance and would benefit from more of it. Those who don't have it are usually less efficient than they might be. They're fatigued, they run out of energy easily, they're depressed, they have less initiative, and they don't have the zest for life they had when they were younger. In a real sense, endurance brings back a certain youthfulness—both physically and mentally.

Endurance is not a guaranteed result of training. But it can be assured when training is done effectively, which always means building the aerobic system. If your main focus is developing only the anaerobic system, then you may not acquire much endurance, since your aerobic function (fat burning) will be limited.

Endurance Increased aerobic function resulting in nearly unlimited energy.

Overtraining and Undertraining

Using the training equation, it's easy to see what happens to many people: either they overtrain because their workouts are excessive or they don't rest enough, or they undertrain because they don't work out enough. In my experience in private practice and in observing people it's clear that the majority of Americans either overtrain or undertrain. Unfortunately, there are too few in the middle. It is my hope that you will seek this important balance.

Much overtraining can be blamed on the "no pain, no gain" myth. According to this myth, you have to suffer, to exercise to the point of agony, in order to benefit from exercise. Too many people begin an exercise program with the clear intention of getting into shape only to get injured and never work out again. You can build your aerobic system with easy exercise, and if you never work out hard, you'll still reap great benefits. For example, dramatic benefits can be attained by easy walking for 30 minutes five days per week. Even if you want to do more, such as run a marathon, it will require additional training, but never to the point of pain.

Probably the main reason why many people don't work out and remain undertrained is that they think it's supposed to be painful, difficult, and complex. Of course some people are just lazy or have different priorities. I've found that the best way to get someone to start regular exercise is through education. When people understand about burning fat—how easy it is to increase their energy and endurance—they're usually hooked.

Others are embarrassed because they really don't have any idea how to start training. They think that everyone knows about working out, and they are afraid to walk into a gym, where they expect to find only power bodies and mirrors. They may have been told by their doctor, who in all likelihood knows as little as they do about exercise, to start a program but not given individualized guidelines.

If you're unsure about how to start, or what to do, begin walking several times a week. There's no simpler way to begin training.

2

Exercise and Stress

> *Excess stress is a common problem in our society, often resulting from combinations and accumulations of stress.*
> *In those who exercise, an imbalance in the training equation typically adds to the problem. And the problem can be exacerbated for the person whose life includes athletic competition.*

Fortunately, most stress conditions can be remedied conservatively. In a sense, that is what this book is about: knowing how to evaluate yourself so that exercise can be a means of reducing stress rather than another source of stress. In addition to the quality of one's exercise, diet and nutrition also may play a major role in stress reduction. Too many carbohydrates (especially refined sugar) and too much caffeine, too little food (low-calorie "diets," skipping meals), and a low nutrient intake (relatively common in the United States) are examples.

The focus of this chapter is stress—what it is, why it's important in relation to exercise, and what you can do to keep it from negatively impacting on your program. Two important issues we will consider are how stress is caused by exercise and how stress affects exercise.

Stress can come from anywhere—from your job, your family,

other people, your emotions, infections, allergic reactions, physical trauma and exertion, even the weather. Stress can be defined as any influence on the body or the mind to which we react, and our reaction may even include an attempt to adapt to it. This reaction and adaptation are mediated through the nervous system by the adrenal glands, which are located on top of the kidneys. Among the important roles of the adrenals is helping the body to recover from exercise. But all adaptation takes time and energy, and the more stress you experience, the more time and energy it takes to adapt.

Remember that not all stress is negative; stress can have a positive outcome. Stress that has a positive outcome is known as *eustress*. Exercise is a good example. As a result of being mildly stressed over time and adapting to this stress, your body performs better. But that same stressor—your workout—can become negative if you go too far beyond the body's ability to recover from it, creating a training imbalance.

Stress can be physical, chemical, or mental-emotional. While most of us are familiar with mental or emotional stress, the other two often are not associated. Mental stress may include tension, anxiety, and depression. Unrealistic goals or no goals at all are also stresses. Mental and emotional stress can also be referred to as behavioral stress—and they don't just occur in children.

Another common mental stress is obsession. I'm not talking about compulsive disorders or extreme problems but the milder forms of obsessions many of us have. These "mental fixations" can turn quite irrational, especially when it comes to exercise. For example, go to a typical health club and what do you see? Mirrors. People want to see what they look like on the outside, but often they don't think about what they're doing to their insides. Then there are the compulsive exercisers, who fear that if they take a day off, they will lose all they have gained. This is the case in those who are overtrained. Counting miles, a tradition with runners, can also work against you. A runner who has 38 miles at week's end but has to squeeze in 2 more miles just to get to 40, even though he or she is tired, has an unhealthy obsession, as does the runner who includes in the week's total the 80 meters jogged between his or her car and the office twice daily.

We have already discussed the most common type of physical

stress—exercise. But lack of activity, poor posture, bad shoes, and dental stress are other frequently encountered types.

Chemical stress includes poor nutrition, dehydration, and too much caffeine. The health and fitness of much of our body, including the nervous system and the brain, the muscles, and the intestines, is controlled by chemistry, so that these areas are especially sensitive to chemical stress.

An important feature of stress is that it is cumulative. Too much exercise on the weekend may be amplified by Monday's mental work stress and further compounded by a mental family stress on Tuesday. This could have a negative impact on your Thursday workout.

Weather is also a potential stressor, and some people are more vulnerable to this stress than others. Exercising in extreme temperatures or humidity, when the barometric pressure is very low, or in full sun can be very stressful. Seasonal affective disorder (SAD) is a good example of a symptom of weather stress (see chapter 14): in the fall and winter, when daylight is diminished and cooler temperatures prevail, some people become depressed or just feel very "sluggish." (One therapy involves being exposed to a source of full-spectrum light, which can be accomplished by spending some time outdoors and using special light bulbs inside.)

Some people have a greater ability to tolerate stress. This may have to do with efficient adrenal glands (and a balanced nervous system, since this works

Stressed Out? Any of These Sound Familiar?

The following symptoms are common in those who are not adapting well to stress; see the following pages for explanations:

- *Low energy*
- *Dizziness upon standing*
- *Eyes sensitive to light*
- *Asthma and allergies*
- *Problems in the low back, knee, foot, and ankle*
- *The problems referred to as burnout, overtraining, and nervous breakdown*
- *Blood sugar problems*
- *Insomnia*
- *Diminished sexual drive*
- *Seasonal affective disorder (SAD)*

closely with the adrenals). Then again, too much stress can reduce the efficiency of these systems.

Effects of Excess Stress

In order to understand how too much stress adversely affects your exercise program, it's first necessary to understand what the adrenal glands really do. That's because excess stress can render the adrenals less effective in their vital job in keeping you healthy and fit.

The adrenal glands are essential for life, and they impact the body through the action of their hormones. There are four types of adrenal hormones; for simplicity, we'll call them type 1 (the glucocorticoids), type 2 (the mineralcorticoids), type 3 (the sex hormones), and type 4 (the catacholamines).

Type 1 includes a key stress hormone called *cortisol*. Cortisol, which acts as a powerful natural anti-inflammatory, is needed daily for all types of recovery, especially recovery from exercise. Whether you take a 30-minute walk or spend the day at the office or working on your word processor, your body produces inflammation. The more intense the activity or exercise, the more inflammation is produced. Without the adrenals' control over this process, the inflammation would persist, ultimately causing chronic problems. Cortisol also has other functions; notably, it helps make fat and sugar more available for energy and stimulates protein utilization, which is necessary for repair and recovery.

The other three groups of hormones also have some important functions. Type 2 hormones help regulate our electrolytes, especially sodium and potassium, which helps prevent dehydration. The type 3 hormones, which include estrogen, progesterone, and testosterone, help both males and females with sexual function and reproduction, as well as muscle and bone repair and development. DHEA (dehydroepiandrosterone, a precursor to estrogen and testosterone production) is another type 3 hormone. The type 4 hormones, epinephrine (sometimes referred to as adrenaline) and norepinephrine, help regulate the rate and power of the heartbeat, increase sugar and fat burning, and improve circulation in the muscles.

Stress causes the adrenal glands to produce more of certain hormones and less of others. If this occurs too intensely or too frequently, it can lead to hormonal imbalance. For example, too much cortisol is the most common response to any stress. If the level of this hormone increases too much, it can suppress the immune system, which lowers the body's defense mechanism, making one more susceptible to colds, flu, and other infections. This is why some people get sick following a hard or long workout, especially following a competition. In addition, excess cortisol can increase the body's sugar-burning mechanism at the expense of fat burning. In short, too much stress can reduce fat burning.

The table below identifies some important adrenal hormones and their actions.

HORMONE	ACTION
Type 1 (glucocorticoids)	anti-inflammatory, increases fat and sugar burning, promotes protein use
Type 2 (mineralcorticoids)	regulates electrolytes and water
Type 3 (sex hormones)	regulates sexual function, muscle and bone support
Type 4 (epinephrine and norepinephrine)	improves blood flow to muscles, promotes fat and sugar burning

The adrenal glands function like clockwork, an activity referred to as your circadian rhythm. Traveling east and west through time zones produces a type of stress called *jet lag*. You stay on your previous time schedule until the adrenal glands adapt to the stress, which may take two or three days or longer.

Stages of the Stress Reaction

Our knowledge about stress and adrenal function began in the early part of this century, when a young medical student named Hans Selye began to piece together the triad of common signs resulting from excess stress: enlargement of the adrenal glands, depressed immunity, and intestinal dysfunction. Selye called it the General Adaptation Syndrome, or GAS. The effects of stress reaction, it was eventually discovered, extend throughout the body.

▶ The alarm reaction, *an increase in the production of some adrenal hormones, is the first response to stress. Stress, which can be compensated for with the help of rest, can prove healthy. The alarm reaction occurs in many people when they first start an exercise program. In a sense, almost any program will return some benefits in the short term, even a program that would ultimately result in overtraining if it were followed for too long a time. The alarm reaction is an attempt by the adrenals to battle the increased stress. This battle is usually successful, and adrenal function returns to normal. But if the alarm reaction continues, a variety of mild symptoms may occur: tiredness during the day, mild allergies, or even some nagging back, knee, or foot pain. Many of these seemingly minor symptoms (sometimes considered to be a normal part of working out) are clues from your body that more recovery is needed or that the total level of stress may be too high. If, over time, the adrenals are unable to successfully battle the stress, they enter the second phase.*

▶ The resistance stage *is the second response to stress. The whole gland enlarges in an attempt to further increase hormone production to counter the stress. During this stage more symptoms develop or new ones appear, including fatigue, insomnia, and more serious back, knee, or foot pain. If the stress continues, the adrenals can become exhausted.*

The General Adaptation Syndrome

- *Alarm reaction: increased adrenal hormone production*
- *Resistance stage: enlargement of the adrenal glands*
- *Exhaustion stage: inability of the adrenal glands to adapt to stress*

▶ *The exhaustion stage is just that: extreme fatigue. The adrenal gland is unable to adapt to stress, and all hormone output is greatly reduced. At this point the person usually becomes more seriously ill—physically, chemically, or mentally.*

Obviously, symptoms such as fatigue, insomnia, and musculoskeletal pain can also have other causes. However, in many individuals adrenal dysfunction is a primary cause of these problems.

Most people who cannot effectively handle stress remain in the first or second stage; only a few enter the third stage. In general, the following symptoms are common in those who are not adapting well to stress:

▶ **Low energy.** *People typically experience low energy in the afternoon, but it could be at any time of day, and in some cases it is all the time. This fatigue can be physical or mental (typically in the form of diminished concentration). When the adrenals are too stressed, the body uses more sugar and less fat for energy.*

▶ **Dizziness upon standing.** *People become dizzy upon standing after bending down to pick something off the floor because not enough blood reaches the head quickly enough following this postural change. Check your blood pressure when you are lying down and then immediately after you stand. Your systolic pressure (the first number) should increase when you're standing by about 6 to 8 mm. In cases of extreme adrenal stress, the pressure either does not increase enough or decreases.*

▶ **Eyes sensitive to light.** *Adrenal stress often causes increased light sensitivity. You may need to wear sunglasses, or you may find night driving difficult because of the oncoming headlights. You may even misinterpret your condition as bad night vision. In some people nearsightedness (the inability to see at a distance) worsens with adrenal dysfunction.*

▶ **Asthma and allergies.** *Asthma and allergies are often associated with poor adrenal function. Sometimes asthmatic symptoms don't appear until the onset of exercise (exercise-induced* asthma). Allergies are often seasonal if pollen or mold related. Allergies can also be associated with certain foods.

▶ **Musculoskeletal symptoms.** Problems in the low back, knee, foot, and ankle are often associated with excess stress. This may be due to the inability of the body to produce enough anti-inflammatory hormones, but it may also result from a lack of muscle support in these areas. It has been clinically observed that muscles associated with these areas can malfunction when adrenal stress is high.

▶ **Stress-related syndromes.** The problems referred to as burnout, overtraining, and nervous breakdown are often the result of adrenal exhaustion.

▶ **Problems handling blood sugar.** For years people have talked about low blood sugar. Accurate indicators of low blood sugar are often difficult to obtain in part because this condition is usually secondary to adrenal dysfunction. This low blood sugar syndrome typically produces symptoms of hunger or irritability before meals or when meals are delayed, as well as strong cravings for sweets and/or caffeine.

▶ **Insomnia.** Falling asleep easily (quite often because of exhaustion) but then waking in the middle of the night, seemingly with lots of energy, and having difficulty getting back to sleep is typical of adrenal dysfunction. This may be due to high cortisol, which during sleeping hours should be low. (Many people say they wake up to urinate, but it's usually the adrenal problem that awakens them first, followed by the urge to urinate.)

▶ **Diminished sexual drive.** People with a low sex drive usually have reduced levels of sex hormones. Eventually this condition can also adversely affect the strength of bones and muscles (i.e., from low estrogen and testosterone). Unfortunately, DHEA taken as a supplement can often have serious health repercussions, including further hormonal imbalance, if it is not prescribed properly (it can result in further reduction of natural DHEA).

▶ **Seasonal affective disorder (SAD).** *As the hours of daylight lessen and the temperature drops, many people seem to go into a mild hibernation. Their metabolism slows, and their body and mind become sluggish, sometimes resulting in feelings of depression, with weight gain a common occurrence. This usually corresponds with adrenal dysfunction. Contributing to this dilemma may be a combination of stresses: the weather, lack of sunlight, and even the start of the holiday season. People don't eat as well as they intend, and they exercise less.*

It should be noted that this discussion about adrenal dysfunction does not include adrenal disease, in which a complete shutdown can occur. This is called Addison's disease, which if not treated medically results in death.

Your Stress List

The key to controlling stress is to first carefully assess it, with the goal of diminishing or eliminating as much excess and unwanted stress as possible. For many people, exercise is a major player in stress: they exercise too much, too intensively, or too little.

Here is a technique I have used successfully for many patients:

1. *First, evaluate your individual stresses. Write them down. Include separate columns for your physical, chemical, and mental stresses. The list will take several days to complete since you won't think of all your different stresses right away.*

2. *Next, separate your list into two parts, "A" and "B." The "A" list should comprise the stresses you can control, such as unhealthy exercise habits as described throughout this book. The "B" list should comprise the stresses you can't control, at least not realistically, such as job stress or the weather. In reality, almost any stress can be modified or eliminated. It's a question of how far you want to go to be healthier and more fit.*

3. Beginning with your "A" list, circle your three biggest stresses from this list and begin to work on them. You may be able to improve on some and totally eliminate others. Changing many stresses may require habit changes, so it could take two or three weeks of concentration. It's a big task, but one that will return great benefits. As you succeed in eliminating or modifying each one, cross it off your list and circle the next most stressful one so that you always have three to work on. With regard to the items on the "B" list, if there's nothing you can do about them, then don't worry about them. Take them out of your mind. Many people expend lots of energy on stresses they can't or won't do anything about. If you

---

Simple Ways to Avoid Stress

You're probably familiar with other strategies for dealing with stress, though you may not use them. Here's a reminder:

- Learn to say "no" when asked to do something you really don't want to do. Running longer or faster than you want because everyone else is doing it can be a major stress.
- Decide not to waste your time worrying about the past or the future. That's not to say that you should ignore the past or not plan for the future. It's important to have goals. And if you've not been consistent with your exercise, so be it. It's never too late to make a new beginning.
- Learn some relaxation techniques and perform them regularly. Even if you normally run or bike, an easy walk by yourself can be a great opportunity for meditation.
- When you're concerned about something, talk it over with someone you trust. An exercise partner can be great as long as he or she does not add to your stress.
- Simplify your life. Start by eliminating trivia: get in the habit of asking yourself, "Is this really important?"
- Prioritize your busy schedule: do the most important things first. But don't neglect the enjoyable things. Before getting out of bed in the morning, decide what fun things you'll do today—including exercise.

The Maffetone Method

work on the stress you can modify and stop worrying about those you can't, your adrenal glands will have a much easier time of managing your overall stress. As time goes on, you may get to your "B" list. You'll realize that changing jobs is a must, for example, or that moving to a more compatible climate is necessary for your health.

Exercises That Increase Stress

Stress is somewhat relative. An exercise that provides a great workout for one person can be a terrible stress for another. In developing an exercise program it is important to consider the needs of your body. You need to find the right type of exercise, as well as the proper duration and intensity of each workout, for your body. If you do not match your body's needs properly, you most likely will create too much stress. Throughout this book there are specific items to help you accomplish this task.

The most common exercise stress is not a particular exercise but rather the intensity at which it is performed. Specifically, anaerobic exercise can be a major stress on the body. Although exercises such as walking, running, biking, aerobic dance, and others can be aerobic, they can also be anaerobic if the intensity is too high. In addition, some exercise is strictly anaerobic even when it is done at a slower pace. Such anaerobic exercises include weight lifting (free weights) and using weight/power machines such as Nautilus, Soloflex, and others that require you to use power. Sit-ups and push-ups, the most traditional of morning workouts, are also anaerobic.

Chapters 5 and 6 discuss this issue in more detail and also explain how you can determine if your potentially aerobic workouts are really anaerobic. It's as simple as measuring your heart rate. In general, aerobic workouts are easier; when you've completed an aerobic session, you should feel that you could do the same workout again and still have fun.

Anaerobic workouts must be balanced with aerobic ones, as discussed in chapter 1. But you should also be aware of anaerobic stimulation, which can come from any stress, because it affects your aerobic/anaerobic balance. In other words, too much stress from any source can stimulate your anaerobic system, possibly causing too much anaerobic and too little aerobic function. Consider a hard day at the office. You're trying to make deadlines, there are too many phone calls, and you feel pressure from the boss or clients. These things put as much stress on your adrenal glands and nervous system as a hard run, a weight lifting session, or competition.

Here's another factor to consider: when outlining your exercise plan, it's important to note which workouts are aerobic and which are anaerobic. Included in your list of stresses might also be your anaerobic training. And if your nonexercise stress is high, an anaerobic workout may be the last thing you need. Anaerobic workouts may be added after aerobic function is developed.

What is more important, anaerobic stress beyond what you can compensate for can diminish your aerobic potential and related function, such as fat burning. There may be several reasons for this.

- *Like other stresses placed on the adrenal glands, anaerobic activity significantly increases the level of cortisol, which shifts your body's energy source from fat burning to sugar burning.*

- *Training results in the development of specific muscle fibers— both aerobic and anaerobic. Too much anaerobic training can result in fewer aerobic muscle fibers.*

- *More time spent training your anaerobic system means less time devoted to building good aerobic function.*

- *Hard workouts produce lactic acid, which may have an adverse effect on the chemistry of your aerobic muscles, rendering them less effective.*

It's relatively easy to measure your aerobic function, as described in chapter 7, and, more important, to determine if and when stress is having an adverse effect on it.

Anaerobic training can lead to some specific problems not usually associated with aerobic workouts:

- *Muscle injuries almost always occur in the anaerobic muscle fibers.*

- *Maintaining anaerobic training for long periods can lead to "staleness" and a plateau in exercise benefits.*

- *Overtraining is strongly associated with anaerobic training.*

- *Unlike aerobic training, anaerobic training does not improve long-term fat-burning ability.*

Stress Testing

Your doctor may want you to take a stress test before starting a program or for any other reason he or she deems necessary. This is a screening procedure used to evaluate the heart under the stress of exercise. Most stress tests employ a treadmill, a bicycle ergometer, or a step machine.

Your doctor should not make any decision based solely on a stress test; rather, the stress test should be part of an overall evaluation that includes at least a physical exam, blood tests, and an electrocardiogram (ECG or EKG). About 30 percent of persons with normal ECGs have heart disease, and about 80 percent of these cases can be diagnosed by administering a stress test. In addition, a stress test may uncover hidden hypertension in someone whose blood pressure is normal when the body is at rest. During exercise, the blood pressure normally rises. But an exaggerated increase may indicate future hypertension.

According to the American College of Sports Medicine, persons over the age of 35 who show evidence of heart disease or have a significant combination of risk factors should be tested. Primary risk factors include hypertension, high blood cholesterol or triglycerides, and cigarette smoking. Secondary risk factors include a family history of heart disease, obesity, or diabetes. Generally, a stress test is not recommended for persons under the age of 35 with no evidence of significant primary or secondary risk factors.

Even people who exercise regularly should pay attention to any signs or symptoms of possible heart disease. In 30 percent of cases the initial manifestation of heart disease is accompanied by angina pectoris, chest pain usually in the upper chest, but the pain often is displayed in the left shoulder or arm, the neck, or the jaw (although usually on the left, this can sometimes occur on the right side). It's triggered by a low level of blood and oxygen through the coronary artery, the main blood vessel of the heart. The symptom usually begins during activity and subsides with rest.

Stress tests aren't highly accurate. About 25 percent of tests give false-negative results, meaning that the test has failed to uncover an existing problem. Fifteen percent of tests give false-positive results, meaning that they indicate a problem that doesn't exist. Thus, 60 percent of the tests are accurate. This is why other tests should be performed in conjunction with a stress test. And a good history, followed by a physical exam, is the first step in a complete evaluation.

3

The Structural, Chemical, and Mental Aspects of Exercise

Employing the right exercise for your body's needs and creating a balanced training program can significantly help you in three important ways— structurally, chemically, and mentally.

Structural Benefits

The benefits of exercise to the body's physical structure are most well known; exercise contributes to not only muscle development but also bone and joint strength, improved posture, and increased ability to withstand physical and other stresses.

Exercise stresses the muscles, making them stronger. As discussed in chapter 2, too much stress can cause muscle injuries. Many aerobic exercises do not lead to dramatic bulking of muscles. Some people, especially women, avoid exercise because they don't want bulky muscles. This is another misconception about exercise.

Exercise can improve muscle power without the bulking up so

common in weight lifters. Aerobic exercise makes muscles work better but doesn't make them get too large. However, because of the fat-burning benefits of aerobic training, body fat is reduced and your muscles become more evident. This gives you the more sculptured, natural look that most people prefer to the bulk from lifting weights. Many people lift weights to try and obtain this sculptured, natural look, but if they don't reduce their body fat sufficiently, there will always be some fat covering the muscles, and they'll never look sculptured.

As mentioned in chapter 2, aerobic muscle fibers are the ones that support our bones and joints, protecting us from injury and damage from aging and physical strain. This benefit by itself is enough reason for most people to pay more attention to developing the aerobic muscle fibers. In addition, exercise strengthens bones because of the gravity stress placed upon them. Exercises that are non–weight bearing and therefore induce less gravity stress are less effective in strengthening bones. Therefore, walking, jogging, running, aerobics, and stair machines are examples of workouts that can strengthen bones. Swimming, cycling, and machines that don't induce some gravity stress are less effective in strengthening bones, although they provide an equally effective aerobic workout. For individuals who have injuries, especially to the bone (such as a stress fracture), or those with weak bones or other vulnerabilities non-weight-bearing exercises are better for rehabilitation.

Another important physical benefit of exercise is the development of more blood vessels. This allows more blood to bring more oxygen and nutrients to more areas of the body and to eliminate more of the waste products that are continuously being produced, even when the body is at rest. In people who don't exercise and are inactive a significant number of existing blood vessels shut down because they have no reason—no stimulation from exercise or activity—to work.

Other Structural Aspects of Exercise

Other structural aspects of exercise to consider include the shoes you wear, the surface you work out on, and other gear (such as light weights or bike gears).

Which shoes to wear when you exercise is the most important structural consideration of exercise. This issue is addressed more fully in chapter 15. For now, however, it should be noted that the three primary things to consider when choosing shoes are how they fit, what they are made of, and how thick the soles are. Many people wear shoes that are too small, and many shoes can contribute to injury because they provide too much support and their soles are too thick and cushiony.

The terrain on which you walk, run, dance, or perform other workouts becomes secondary once the proper shoe is worn. In general, the more natural the surface, the safer it is. For example, a wooden gym floor is a more natural surface than concrete. Natural surfaces are generally safer because they "give" more when your weight places stress upon them, while concrete and steel, for example, have very little "give." This makes the body's reaction to the natural surface quite normal but its reaction to the unnatural material more stressful. The best exercise surface, because the most natural, may be dirt—a soccer field, for example. Working out on concrete and steel may induce the most physical stress.

Some people add light weights to their walking, jogging, or dancing workout. The idea behind this is to increase stress in order to increase the exercise benefits. However, since most people already induce too much exercise stress, adding more weight may be counterproductive. The best way to determine whether added weight will help you is to check your heart rate (see chapter 6). If you use weights, they should be very light: begin with an 8-ounce weight and increase to no more than 1.5 pounds in each hand.

Chemical Benefits

When exercise improves your health and fitness, it's due as much to the chemical benefits it imparts as to the structural benefits, and sometimes the chemical benefits outweigh the structural. Among the chemical benefits the most important are the metabolic improvements gained through aerobic exercise, specifically the increase in long-term fat burning and the diminished reliance on sugar for energy.

If you add up the calories burned during a workout, you'll see that the harder you exercise, the more calories you burn. This might lead you to conclude that you will burn more fat if you train anaerobically than you will if you train aerobically since the total number of calories burned during, say, one hour of hard training will exceed the number burned during one hour of aerobic exercise. However, hard workouts program your metabolism to rely more on sugar and less on fat for energy and in the long run will result in less total fat burned during the other 23 hours of the day. In the hours following an aerobic workout you'll be teaching your body to burn more fat than you will after an anaerobic workout. In other words, anaerobic training doesn't program your body for long-term fat burning as aerobic training does.

Another important benefit of building the aerobic muscle fibers is that they contain a significant proportion of the body's antioxidant activity. Most people know that antioxidant vitamins and minerals control free radicals, which tear the body down, speed up aging, and may lead to diseases such as cancer and heart disease. Not only do anaerobic muscle fibers lack the antioxidant activity of aerobic fibers but anaerobic exercise significantly increases the number of free radicals.

A well-developed aerobic muscle system helps to keep the body well hydrated. Dehydration is a common problem in people who exercise, especially athletes who train for long hours and compete. The aerobic muscle fibers maintain a much higher level of hydration than do the anaerobic fibers.

Other Chemical Factors

In order for your body to reap the benefits of aerobic training, the aerobic muscle fibers require sufficient iron. Persons who are anemic or whose iron level is even mildly low may not benefit as much as they might from aerobic training. That does not mean, however, that everyone should take iron supplements. An excess of iron, which is stored in the body as ferritin, has been associated with heart disease. A simple blood test can evaluate the level of iron, along with the levels of hemoglobin and hematocrit, in your blood; and the ferritin level indicates how much iron is stored in your body, including the amount of iron in the aerobic muscles.

Your diet also can influence how much benefit you obtain from working out. For example, too much sugar, especially if it is eaten right before exercise, can reduce your fat-burning ability. (This very complex issue is discussed more fully in chapter 20.)

Mental Benefits

Exercise should be fun. If it's a chore, something probably isn't right: your workouts may be too long or too intense, or you may not have the right training partner. If it isn't fun, look for the reason and correct it. Having fun is a great benefit of exercise, especially when other things are tough—when work is not going great, or you have personal stresses, or it's the dead of winter.

Separate from the enjoyment and at the same time an important part of it is the meditation that training can provide, especially when you work out alone or when you don't feel pressured to talk to those around you. Time may seem different, you feel as if both your body and mind are flowing, sometimes you even feel as though you're leaving your body—it's truly a meditative experience.

On a more concrete level, aerobic training, because it relies less on sugar burning and therefore helps to keep your blood sugar levels stable, can help keep your brain mentally more stable too. Rapid changes in blood sugar levels or levels that are too low (which is not uncommon when the body can't get enough energy from fat) can make you feel depressed.

Other Mental Factors

Knowing that you're doing something right and good for yourself is a reward in itself. When your program is balanced, you will tend to be consistent rather than starting and stopping, as so often is the case with people who work out. And especially when you notice the myriad of physical benefits you are deriving from proper exercise, your mental state will improve.

Encouragement is vital to maintaining your program. Some people find encouragement by joining a gym, others read books to learn about exercise, and still others are encouraged by their personal success. Research shows that encouragement not only helps people continue exercising but reduces the incidence of disease.

4

Developing Maximum Aerobic Function

From proper aerobic exercise the body will derive a very efficient cardiovascular system (the heart, lungs, and circulation), very high levels of bone and joint support and body-fat burning, as well as other benefits. These benefits can be derived from many types of exercise, including walking, stationary biking, aerobic dance, using the stair machine, jogging, biking, swimming, and others, when simple guidelines are followed. Unfortunately, many people who think they are getting these long-term benefits are not. The specific focus of this chapter is how to build the aerobic system to obtain maximum aerobic function, or MAF.

Increased aerobic function means increased aerobic muscle fiber development, improved fat burning, antioxidant benefits, and other benefits described in previous chapters. Most important, you'll need to work smartly, not hard, to obtain these benefits. You'll have to plan your schedule and set priorities.

The most important part of your schedule is the *aerobic base,* the time you'll need to spend to build your aerobic system. During this period of time you'll perform only aerobic exercise; there will be no anaerobic training. This aerobic base period can last three to five months, sometimes longer.

How do you know when you've built a sufficient aerobic base? Among the best ways are measuring your heart rate during exercise and utilizing the MAF test (both are discussed in chapters 6 and 7). An effective way to measure aerobic development is to calculate how much fat your body burns. Body-fat levels begin to decrease when aerobic function improves. By measuring your body-fat content you can determine whether your body is burning fat efficiently. Weighing yourself on the scale is not the best way to do this, but the use of a tape measure is ideal.

Measuring Fat Burning

As mentioned in chapter 1, a gas analyzer can determine how much fat and sugar are burned during exercise at various levels of intensity and when the body is at rest (although not during exercise at maximum intensity). But although this technique is simple, it is not readily available to most people. A method that is not only simple but sufficiently accurate (much more than the scale when it comes to body fat) is to use a tape measure. The best places to measure are your waist and hips.

The waist-to-hip ratio cannot determine the percentage of fat in your body. The actual number is less

---

Top Reasons for Increased Body Fat

Dietary imbalance

Increased stress

Too much food

Too little food (which can reduce metabolism)

Too much dietary carbohydrate

Too much dietary fat

Too few essential dietary fats

Too little physical activity

Too much anaerobic exercise

Why Build an Aerobic Base?

A variety of benefits result from building an aerobic base. Here are the 10 most important:

- *Aerobic muscle fibers are very resistant to injury. When a person is injured, it's usually the anaerobic fibers that are damaged. And joint support comes from aerobic fibers.*
- *Persons with better aerobic development are less likely to become dehydrated.*
- *Fat burning takes place in the aerobic muscle fibers; the more they are developed, the more fat you'll burn.*
- *Aerobic muscles provide endurance not only for exercise but for all physical and mental activity. Even in a marathon, 99 percent of one's energy comes from the aerobic system (see the chart on the next page).*
- *Aerobic speed—the ability to work faster and harder with the same or less energy—can be developed only when one has a high level of aerobic function.*
- *Increased aerobic function improves circulation and the functioning of the whole cardiovascular system.*
- *The increased blood circulation in the aerobic muscles helps the nearby anaerobic fibers work better when sprint or added power is needed. This is vital for weight lifters.*
- *Antioxidant activity—so necessary to optimal health—takes place in the aerobic muscles.*
- *High levels of aerobic function almost assure that you won't be overtrained.*
- *Persons who develop their aerobic system usually say that exercise is more fun.*

important than whether it's diminishing. As aerobic function improves, the body-fat content will lessen, and this will manifest itself in smaller waist and hip measurements.

Devices for measuring body fat, such as calipers and the many other gadgets now on the market, are only general indicators of body-fat content, and their outcomes are not consistent. The waist-to-hip ratio, however, can tell you much more about your body fat.

It can provide clues about whether your body-fat content is heavily influenced by diet.

The ratio is determined by dividing the waist circumference, measured at the level of your umbilicus (belly button), by the hip circumference, measured at the level where your hips are widest.

$$Waist\text{-}to\text{-}hip\ ratio = \frac{waist}{hips}$$

A ratio above 0.9 in men and 0.8 in women may indicate that a significant proportion of body fat comes from excess carbohydrates in the diet, especially the refined type found in bagels and all sugar (especially sugar hidden in foods). Persons on low-fat diets in order to lose weight usually eat significantly more carbohydrates than those who are not on these diets (see chapter 20).

Most important, the waist-to-hip ratio is useful for evaluating whether your aerobic system is developing properly. If that is the case, your ratio will gradually diminish, along with your excess fat stores. This is an excellent method of monitoring your aerobic base development. Measure yourself once per month, on the same calendar date (for example, on the first of each month). Do not measure yourself more often. The changes are not noticeable from day to day, and taking daily measurements can make you obsessive, much like the person who gets on the scale each morning and becomes depressed, skips meals, or overtrains if he or she weighs one pound more than the day before.

AEROBIC AND ANAEROBIC CONTRIBUTIONS TO ENERGY

DURATION OF ACTIVITY (MINUTES)	% AEROBIC	% ANAEROBIC
2	50	50
4	65	35
10	85	15
30	95	5
60	98	2
120	99	1

Work output is maximum effort for 2, 4, 10, etc., minutes. For example, in a 30-minute, all-out effort, 95% of the energy comes from the aerobic system.

5

Developing the Anaerobic System

I am not opposed to anaerobic exercise per se, which involves working out at a high heart rate while walking, running, dancing, cycling, rowing, or performing some other exercise. Even lifting weights, which is always anaerobic, could serve an important purpose in a well-designed program. However, you must always keep in mind the concept of balance.

I *am* opposed to anaerobic training if it causes an imbalance. Knowing when and if to add anaerobic workouts to your program is the key to making it work for you rather than against you. But the fact is that the majority of people I have trained, even many world-class and professional athletes, did not require anaerobic additions to their training schedule. Moreover, most injuries and overtraining occur in those performing anaerobic training.

Anaerobic Training

Whether it's through higher-intensity walking, running, biking, dancing, or similar workouts or by using weight lifting and other gym equipment, you can effectively develop your anaerobic system with proper exercise. Among the machines you might use are rowing machines, stair devices, treadmills, and the various cycling machines available.

The most important aspect of anaerobic training is knowing when to add it to your program. The worst time to do this is at the onset. If you've never worked out, or if you have not exercised regularly, the first thing to do is build your aerobic system. Anaerobic training, as I've defined it, will not build your aerobic system. The only exception is if you're working closely with a professional and plan to use anaerobic exercise only to jump-start your metabolism—in this case, it is only used for three or four weeks.

Whatever the case, when starting anaerobic training pay close attention to these rules:

▶ *Never train anaerobically more than two to three times each week, and separate anaerobic sessions by at least 48 hours to assure good recovery. If your workout schedule includes six or seven days each week, at most three anaerobic sessions are acceptable; if you work out four to five days each week, two anaerobic days are more appropriate; if you work out only three days each week, only one of these sessions should be anaerobic; and if you work out fewer than three days each week, anaerobic workouts are not recommended since it would be too easy to create an imbalance.*

▶ *Always include aerobic workouts with your anaerobic training, keeping in mind the following:*

- *All anaerobic training should be preceded by an easy aerobic warm-up and followed by an easy aerobic cooldown.*
- *On the days between anaerobic exercise, perform an easy aerobic workout.*

As long as you continue to feel good and do not become exhausted or injured, continue your anaerobic training for up to one month. Most people can attain significant anaerobic benefits after a month's worth of these workouts. Training anaerobically for longer periods increases the risk of creating an aerobic-anaerobic imbalance followed by the aerobic system suppression.

For most people, the anaerobic workout itself (not including the warm-up and cooldown) should last from 20 to 45 minutes. Your workout should last longer than this only if you are in competition, whether as a runner, a biker, a triathlete, or a weight lifter.

Anaerobic training may require more recovery. For some, this means more days off from training.

Many people continue anaerobic training because they think it will bring them benefits that can only be attained through aerobic workouts.

Sample One-Hour Workouts

6 Days a Week:
Walking, Jogging, Machines, and Weights

▶ *Monday: 15-minute walking warm-up; 30 minutes of weight lifting; 15-minute easy walking cooldown.*

▶ *Tuesday: 60-minute jog.*

▶ *Wednesday: 15-minute walking warm-up; 30 minutes of weight lifting; 15-minute easy walking cooldown.*

▶ *Thursday: 30 minutes on the stair machine; 30 minutes on the treadmill (walk/jog).*

▶ *Friday: 15-minute walking warm-up; 30 minutes of weight lifting; 15-minute easy walking cooldown.*

▶ *Saturday: 30-minute walk.*

▶ *Sunday: off.*

5 Days a Week:
Machines, Jogging, Weights, and Walking

▶ Monday: off.

▶ Tuesday: 60-minute jog.

▶ Wednesday: 15-minute stationary-bike warm-up; 30 minutes of weight lifting; 15-minute easy walking cooldown.

▶ Thursday: 30 minutes on the stair machine; 30 minutes on the treadmill (walk/jog).

▶ Friday: 15-minute stationary-bike warm-up; 30 minutes of weight lifting; 15-minute easy walking cooldown.

▶ Saturday: off.

▶ Sunday: 30-minute walk.

6 Days a Week:
Walking, Jogging, and Running

▶ Monday: 15-minute walk/jog warm-up; 30 minutes of running intervals; 15-minute easy walk/jog cooldown.

▶ Tuesday: 60-minute jog.

▶ Wednesday: 15-minute walk/jog warm-up; 30 minutes of running intervals; 15-minute easy walk/jog cooldown.

▶ Thursday: 60-minute walk/jog.

▶ Friday: 15-minute walk/jog warm-up; 30 minutes of running intervals; 15-minute easy walk/jog cooldown.

▶ Saturday: 60-minute jog.

▶ Sunday: off.

5 Days a Week:
Walking, Jogging, and Running

▶ Monday: off.

▶ Tuesday: 60-minute jog.

▶ *Wednesday: off.*

▶ *Thursday: 15-minute walk/jog warm-up; 30 minutes of running intervals; 15-minute easy walk/jog cooldown.*

▶ *Friday: off.*

▶ *Saturday: 60-minute jog.*

▶ *Sunday: 15-minute walk/jog warm-up; 30 minutes of running intervals; 15-minute easy walk/jog cooldown.*

Build Your Base

The most appropriate time to incorporate anaerobic training is after you've built a good aerobic base. Since increased aerobic function can provide you with almost all the health and fitness benefits you'll need, and since it serves as a "base" for any additional exercise, building a good aerobic base before adding anaerobic training will assure an optimal balance.

For the very small number of athletes who seek to bulk up their muscles, it may be necessary to do much more anaerobic training. In a real sense, they must overtrain to attain that extra level of power and strength, or very large muscles. The techniques that are required for this go beyond the scope of this book.

To persons who choose to engage in a period of anaerobic training, excluding weight lifting, I would make two recommendations: First, don't allow your heart rate to exceed 90 percent of its maximum level at any time during training (chapter 6 explains how to find your maximum heart rate). Second, use the anaerobic burst method of training, sometimes referred to as interval training. If using this technique when running, for example, perform fast-paced running for short periods of time—the shorter the time, the less stress. Here's an example of this method:

1. *Warm up for 15 minutes with easy jogging.*

2. *Run for 10 seconds at a pace faster than that of normal training.*

3. *Jog at an easy pace for 30 seconds.*

4. *Alternate steps 2 and 3 for 20–30 minutes. Do not allow the fast-pace run to become exhausting.*

5. *Cool down (warming up and cooling down are discussed in chapter 8).*

This type of workout can be performed on a bike, roller blades, a stair or rowing machine, or while walking, dancing, or performing other exercises, or it can be performed using combinations of exercises.

When weight lifting (or using other machines that mimic weights), always begin and end the workout with a warm-up and a cooldown. In addition, do not rush your workout. Many people go to the gym when it's crowded and have to compete for the machines. If someone else is waiting their turn, you're likely to do your repetitions too fast and sloppily, which can increase your risk of injury.

Specific weight lifting methods are not discussed in this book because they should be individualized. I encourage you to get one-on-one assistance if you have not had proper weight-training instruction.

Summary of Anaerobic Benefits

Anaerobic exercise may provide some benefits. These include increased oxygen uptake, increased muscle development for more strength, and the development of sprinting speed. However, these potential benefits may come with the potential risk of overtraining and reduced aerobic function.

6

Exercise and Heart Rate

One of the most important aspects of your exercise program is knowing whether your workout is aerobic or anaerobic. While this can be determined in a laboratory or even with a portable gas analyzer, both of these methods are impractical for most people. A much easier approach, one that is relatively simple and accurate since it parallels laboratory data, is to take your heart rate, or pulse.

The level of exercise intensity is one of the main factors determining whether your body gets an aerobic or an anaerobic workout. Since workout intensity directly affects heart rate, a pulse reading becomes an important tool in quantifying your workout. More specifically, exercise above a certain heart rate is anaerobic, and exercise below that level is aerobic. Knowing the best heart rate for your particular needs is discussed later in this chapter.

Your heart rate can be used in other ways, such as to estimate the number of calories burned during exercise or to estimate oxygen uptake. But the main thing you want to know is whether you're training your body to burn more fat or more sugar. For example, knowing how many calories you burn doesn't tell you how many of those calories come from fat and how many are from sugar. The exercise heart rate can also be related to the blood flow through the coronary artery (the artery that brings blood to the heart muscle), nervous-system function, hormonal function, and other factors, including the mental state.

What is most important is that your heart rate takes the guesswork out of your program. When you know your heart rate, you can determine whether you are training your aerobic or your anaerobic system. Checking your heart rate throughout the workout is ideal, and prevents you from working out anaerobically, which gets you away from fat-burning training.

Measuring Your Heart Rate

There are two methods of obtaining your heart rate. You can measure it manually by feeling your pulse, or you can use an electronic device.

You can take your pulse manually by feeling one of many pulses on the body. The most common and practical ones are the carotid artery pulse, on the front of the neck on either side of the throat, or the radial artery pulse, just above the base of the thumb on the wrist. However, several factors must be considered to assure that an accurate pulse rate is obtained.

1. *Your pulse is best taken by applying light pressure from two or three fingertips. Lightly touch the area of the pulse to perceive the beating artery. The ability to sense this comes with practice, so if you're new to this technique, practice it several times a day to develop accuracy. Light pressure is especially important when using the carotid pulse. Pressing too hard on this area can trigger a slowing of the heart rate, which can result in an inaccurate reading.*

2. *It's important to count properly when taking your pulse. This may sound easy, but you're really counting two different things: the heart rate and the seconds (although this may be accomplished by looking at a watch or listening to someone count off the seconds).*

3. It's common to take your pulse for either 6 or 10 seconds. If you use a 6-second count, multiply the number of beats in 6 seconds by 10. This results in the number of beats per minute (bpm). If you use the 10-second count, multiply the number of beats in 10 seconds by 6. In addition, begin counting from "zero" and not from "one."

4. If you have to stop to take your heart rate, you may obtain an error since stopping causes the heart rate to decrease, sometimes rapidly. In general, if you stop to take your pulse, add 10 beats to the final number when using the 6-second method and 15 beats when using the 10-second method.

	6-SECOND METHOD	10-SECOND METHOD
Total pulse	count heartbeats in 6-second period, multiply by 10	count heartbeats in 10-second period, multiply by 6
When stopping to take pulse	add 10 beats to total	add 15 beats to total

If this sounds too complicated or if you can't be bothered, an option is to obtain your heart rate by wearing a heart rate monitor or clipping one to your ear if you are riding a stationary machine. (Heart rate monitors are discussed in chapter 7.)

Once you find your heart rate, it's important to know whether you're in a fat-burning zone or you're anaerobic. The precise heart rate that keeps you aerobic can be obtained in a laboratory, but there is a formula that you can use that is very accurate and more practical.

220 or 180-Formula?

In the early 1980s I developed a new formula for determining the optimal heart rate for anyone who exercises. This formula, which has proved very successful, is called the *180-Formula*. This replaces the old 220 formulas, which were too inaccurate. The rates obtained using the 180-Formula are generally lower than those obtained using the 220 formulas, which are based on oxygen-consumption tables and estimated maximum heart rates. The 180-Formula is based on each individual's general health and fitness level and was derived from clinical trials and from gas-analyzer results.

It's important that the heart-rate formula take into account the stress of the individual and other health-related factors. For example, when everyday stress is excessive, some people experience changes in their heart-rate response to exercise. Overtrained athletes may experience other changes. These changes can result in a lowering or elevating of the training heart rate. The 180-Formula takes these changes into account because it is adjusted to each person's state of health and fitness. The 220 formulas, however, do not take these changes into account.

The traditional 220 formula relies on two very general indicators:

- *an* estimated *maximum heart rate*

- *training at a specified percentage of that number based on very subjective evidence*

The maximum heart rate is traditionally estimated by subtracting one's age from 220. However, this estimation can vary considerably. The fact is that only some individuals, about one in three, fit this equation. The others have maximum heart rates either above or below this estimated level.

Continuing with the old 220 formula, after you subtract your chronological age from 220, you multiply the difference by a specific percentage. This percentage, which ranges from 65 to 85 percent, represents the percentage of VO_2max (the maximum amount of oxygen our bodies can take from the air we breathe). However, many people use a percentage of the estimated maximum heart rate. These two percentage levels are very different, and people sometimes interchange them. For example, 75 percent of VO_2max corresponds to about 85 percent of the maximum heart rate, and 85 percent of VO_2max corresponds to about 90 percent of the maximum heart rate.

Unfortunately, there is no indication of which percentage to choose, and most people choose the higher option. I have observed that in calculating a training heart rate the percentage most often used is 85 percent, followed by 80 percent; 75 percent is less frequently used, and only a few choose 70 percent or 65 percent. The reason may be that most athletes feel the need to train with more intensity, to follow the "more is better," "no pain, no gain" path.

Another version of the 220 formula is the *Karvonen method*, which takes into account heart-rate reserve. The results of this method correlate with VO_2max but may not be appropriate for all individuals. Research show that this version of the 220 formula is not appropriate for persons with average and low fitness levels.

The 180-Formula

Your optimal heart rate for aerobic training is determined with the 180-Formula as follows:

1. Subtract your age from 180 (180 – age).

2. Modify this number by selecting from the following categories the one that best matches your health and fitness profile:

- *If you are recovering from a major illness (heart disease, any operation, any hospital stay, etc.) or if you are on any regular medication (see below), subtract an additional 10.*
- *If you have not exercised before, have exercised irregularly, have been exercising with injury, have regressed in training or competition, get more than two colds or cases of flu per year, or have allergies or asthma, subtract an additional 5.*
- *If you have been exercising regularly (at least four times weekly) for up to two years without any of the above-mentioned problems, use the (180 – age) number.*
- *If you are a competitive athlete and have been training for more than two years without any of the above-mentioned problems and have made progress in competition without injury, add 5.*

The heart rate obtained by using this formula is referred to as the *maximum aerobic heart rate*.

For example, if you're 30 years old and have not exercised before, then your maximum aerobic heart rate would be 145 bpm, obtained as follows:

$$180 - 30 - 5 = 145$$

If it is difficult to decide which of two categories you belong to, choose the category that gives the lowest maximum aerobic heart rate. If you're taking medication that may affect your heart rate, if you have a pacemaker, or if you have special circumstances not discussed here, further individualization may be necessary with the help of your doctor or another professional.

The 180-Formula may need to be further individualized for those over about age 65. If you're in this age group, you *may* have to add up to 10 beats per minute, depending on your health and fitness levels based on the judgment of a clinical practitioner. For persons 16 years and under, the formula is not applicable; for these persons I have used a heart rate of 165 bpm. A lower heart rate may occasionally be used based on the individual's health and fitness.

Once a maximum aerobic heart rate is found, use a range from that number to 10 beats *below* that number. For example, if your maximum aerobic heart rate is determined to be 155, your *aerobic training zone* would be 145–55 bpm.

It is important to note that persons using this formula for the first time often find that exercise seems too easy. This may be because many people train at very high intensities and/or overtrain. Sometimes persons find that exercise using this formula is too easy because they are programmed according to the "no pain, no gain" myth.

In time, as your aerobic system improves, you'll have to work harder to maintain the same heart rate. This is discussed further in chapter 7; for now you should understand that your exercise pace will change. In time you'll have to go faster. However, you will perceive your exertion to be about the same since you'll still be exercising at the same heart rate.

For example, if you're presently jogging a mile in 12 minutes at a rate of 140 bpm, after three months of training at this heart rate your pace may quicken to 10 minutes per mile. Even though you'll be jogging, or running, faster, you'll be exercising at the same heart rate and feel almost the same as when you were jogging at the slower pace of 12 minutes per mile.

Modifying Your Heart Rate

Once you find your maximum aerobic heart rate and can exercise successfully at that rate, continue to use the same rate for about four to five years *if health and fitness continue to progress*. Then decrease the training rate by about 3 bpm. At that stage your training heart rate may not match the 180-Formula since your overall health and fitness will have improved. Thus, this formula is most beneficial at the start of a program and during periods of great progress. However, if you stop progressing, it may be because your exercise heart rate is too high; in some cases this may be because the 180-Formula was not calculated properly. It is important to be honest and objective in determining your maximum aerobic heart rate.

1

The Use of
Heart Rate Monitors

Today's heart rate monitors are inexpensive and easy to use. They can be cheaper than most moderate or low-end exercise shoes. And if you can drive a car or know how to ride the subway, their use will be easy. I began using heart rate monitors for exercise in the late 1970s, when they were just coming on the market. Today's monitors are cheaper, more streamlined, and even more accurate. Many people find that a heart rate monitor is like a coach, helping them to be more precise about their exercise.

The best heart rate monitors come in two pieces: a thin, narrow belt that straps around the lower chest, which picks up and transmits the heart rate to the second component, a wrist watch. A quick glance at your watch allows you to read your current heart rate. Some, instead of a watch, have an earpiece that tells you the heart rate. Other devices for monitoring your heart rate are less portable, such as monitors that clip on the earlobe or fingertip and devices installed in the grips of some exercise equipment.

A heart monitor may be particularly useful in a number of general situations:

1. *In most cases, a heart monitor helps* limit *exercise intensity in those who may otherwise train at too high a heart rate, which can result in not adequately building the aerobic system. Using a heart monitor also helps prevent overtraining and injury. (The importance of building the aerobic system is discussed in chapter 4.)*

2. *Heart monitors help motivate individuals who may not normally exercise with enough intensity to gain optimal benefits. For example, some studies show that a significant number of patients with coronary heart disease failed to achieve their target heart rate. Sometimes even well-trained athletes do not elevate their heart rate sufficiently despite running, biking, or training at very fast paces.*

3. *A heart monitor can help regulate anaerobic or high-intensity training. A heart rate monitor is a more accurate indicator of one's heart rate than pace, subjective feelings, or even blood lactate measurements (which can fluctuate significantly during hard workouts). For example, during interval running workouts your maximum pace should not exceed 90 percent of your maximum heart rate (which itself can be determined with a heart monitor) except for very brief periods.*

4. *A heart rate monitor can obtain a more accurate heart rate during any exercise than manual methods can. Studies have shown that taking your pulse manually often results in errors. These errors are usually on the side of lower than actual values. Deriving an accurate heart rate count is vital; even exercising at a rate that is 3 or 4 bpm too high can make a significant difference in the quality of your workout and the outcome of your program.*

5. *A heart monitor can measure your progress when used in conjunction with the Maximum Aerobic Function test, discussed on the following pages.*

The Maximum Aerobic
Function Test

By regularly measuring the *time* of a particular activity along with a given *heart rate* and *distance* (or other factors, such as watts) you can monitor your exercise to assure your progress and assess your potential for over- or undertraining. This assessment is referred to as the Maximum Aerobic Function test, or MAF, and may be implemented using almost any training activity—running, walking, biking, stationary apparatus, etc. It is not applicable to weight lifting or similar power activities. For instance, the example in chapter 6— jogging one mile at a heart rate of 140 bpm, initially in 12 minutes—can serve as the basis for a MAF test. A month later the same one-mile jog at the same heart rate takes 11.5 minutes; two months later, 10.5 minutes; and three months later, 10 minutes. This would indicate good progress and also implies increased fat burning. Performing the MAF test monthly, throughout the year, is ideal.

The MAF test is especially useful for noncompetitive individuals, such as those on weight-loss or cardiac-rehabilitation programs, in which improved aerobic function, resulting in increased fat burning, is important. It is also useful for athletes in such sports as basketball, baseball, football, and others that rely on endurance. Any of these individuals can take the MAF test on a treadmill, a track, a stationary bike, or other location.

Excess stress, dietary or nutritional imbalance, or even physical problems may be revealed in the MAF test results. For example, if you progress during the first 12 months of exercise but then see your MAF test results start to worsen, you know that there is a problem. A sudden change for the worse is not normal. You need to discover what the problem is. This may involve consulting a professional. Correction of the problems usually results in a rapid return to improving MAF test times, although in some difficult cases, such as chronic overtraining, restoration to healthy progress may take several weeks or months. Perhaps more important, a MAF

Steady Progress

Jane began a training program of walking that progressed to jogging and running. Her MAF test time initially was about 18.5 minutes per mile. After about ten months Jane was walking faster than 13.5 minutes per mile, and since she found it difficult to walk at that rapid pace, she began jogging. After about a year of jogging, her MAF test time was just under 11 minutes per mile, and six months later it was 9.5 minutes. At that time Jane began participating in local 5- and 10-kilometer road races, and increased her training. Her MAF test time improved to 8 minutes and 45 seconds and remained there for three months. The next month's test was 9 minutes and 15 seconds. After not consulting with me for more than a year, Jane arrived at my office with knee pain, increased fatigue, and depression. She had a number of other overtraining signs and symptoms, including a variety of muscle problems. After three office visits and consequent modifications to her diet and training, Jane began to feel better. During the time of her office visits, her MAF test time remained at 9 minutes and 15 seconds. Two weeks after her first visit, it had improved to about 9 minutes. And after another month she was nearly symptom-free, and her MAF test time had improved to about 8 minutes and 20 seconds; and she continued to make slow but steady improvements.

test result that indicates reduced performance is also an indication that an injury may follow.

Some people choose to perform a longer MAF test. This adds a component of endurance to the test. The chart on the next page shows the progress of a runner who used a heart rate of 145 bpm and a five-mile MAF test.

ACTUAL CASE OF A RUNNER'S 5-MILE MAF TEST IN MINUTES PER MILE

MONTH	MILE 1	MILE 2	MILE 3	MILE 4	MILE 5
April	8:21	8:27	8:38	8:44	8:49
May	8:11	8:18	8:26	8:33	8:39
June	7:57	8:05	8:10	8:17	8:24
July	7:44	7:52	7:59	8:09	8:15

Other MAF Tests

Time, heart rate, and distance can be used in other ways as well. In the examples above, heart rate and distance were the constants and time was the variable. In swimming, heart rate and time can be the constant and the number of laps can be the variable. For example, after an easy warm-up a swimmer maintains a heart rate of 145 bpm and swims for 30 minutes, counting the number of laps covered in that time period. Assuming proper aerobic progress, after several weeks the number of laps completed during the 30-minute period will increase.

To perform a MAF test on a bike, choose a road course that takes about 30 to 45 minutes to complete. After an easy cycling warm-up, ride at your maximum aerobic heart rate and record the total time. As you progress, the time required to complete the course should decrease. For example, it may take 36 minutes and 50 seconds to complete a specific course. A month later, your time may be 35:30 at the same constant heart rate, and in another month, 34:15.

You should perform the MAF test about once a month throughout the year and record the results in your diary. Performing the test more often than that is not recommended as daily or weekly changes may be more difficult to measure objectively; for example, on certain days a temporary worsening may be evident because of variables described below. In addition, focusing on the test too frequently can foster an obsession much like of persons who weigh themselves once or more each day.

One of the great benefits of the MAF test is that it can inform you of potential structural, chemical, or mental obstacles to further progress long before they manifest themselves as injuries or declining exercise benefits. Performing the test irregularly or not often enough reduces your chances of taking advantage of this benefit.

MAF Test Plateau

At some stage of development it is normal for the MAF test time to plateau for a brief period. In other instances, however, a plateau is not normal and reflects some structural, chemical, or mental problem, often a combination of stresses. It is important to distinguish between a normal and abnormal plateau of MAF test results. The following information may be useful.

▶ *A normal plateau typically occurs after approximately six to eight months of progress.*

▶ *When you begin a program, you may continue to progress for a year or more before reaching a plateau.*

▶ *The plateau may last for several weeks but generally no more than one to three months.*

▶ *A longer plateau might be considered abnormal, perhaps indicating the start of a period of overtraining or other problems.*

▶ *In some cases any plateau may be abnormal since various imbalances can cause a halt in progress. Therefore, any plateau should be looked at as possibly indicating a problem.*

Factors That Affect the MAF Test

A number of external factors may cause errors in the MAF test. For runners, for example, the type of track surface may have a slight impact on the pace. Modern high-tech track surfaces result in a slightly faster pace at the same heart rate than cinder or dirt tracks, which slow the pace. A MAF test taken outside on a bike will be affected by the roughness or smoothness of the road surface, its varying grades, and automobile traffic. The pace on hills is usually slower than the pace on flat surfaces unless there are significantly more downhill—as opposed to flat and uphill—sections. A good option is to take the test indoors on a bike with a wind trainer or rollers, especially in climates where weather factors may vary considerably.

Usually these factors and others described below will have a relatively insignificant impact. But in order to make sure that the MAF test is as accurate as possible, use the same course or method each time. In the event that you change the test course, be sure to note it in your diary. In addition, perform the test about the same time each month, as hormonal factors in both men and women may have a slight impact on the test.

Other factors that may interfere with the MAF test include weather, altitude, hydration, food, and equipment. Most of these factors increase your physical effort and your heart rate, forcing you to slow your pace.

The weather can influence the MAF test in several ways:

- *A head wind may physically counter your forward motion, raising your heart rate and slowing your pace. A tailwind will have the opposite effect: you'll go faster at the same rate at which you normally would go without the tailwind.*

- *Extreme heat or extreme cold can raise your heart rate, slowing your pace.*

- *High humidity acts much like a head wind. To work your way through this physical barrier of water you must increase your effort. The increased effort raises your heart rate, causing you to slow down.*

- *Rain and snow have an effect similar to that of humidity or a head wind. Testing in the rain or snow requires more effort. In addition, if the road or track surface is wet, additional physical effort may be required, further raising your heart rate and slowing your pace.*

- *Very low barometric pressure may adversely affect the MAF test, possibly due to a slightly lowered oxygen uptake.*

Often, weather stress is not the result of a single factor. A combination of cold and wind, for example, can elevate the heart rate significantly. The combination of summer heat, humidity, and low barometric pressure can also result in a higher heart rate. For these reasons the MAF test should not be performed when the weather is extreme.

Altitude can have a significant effect on the MAF test, especially if you remain at the higher elevation for too short a period to adapt to the new altitude. If this is the case and it's time to do your MAF test, you should realize that your pace will be slower. If you live at a high altitude and are traveling to *lower* altitudes, your MAF test time will usually improve within the first three weeks.

Hydration also affects body function and can significantly affect the MAF test. In general, even slight dehydration will have a negative effect. Dehydration is perhaps the most common nutritional problem in people who exercise.

Equipment, such as bicycles and their components, other exercise equipment, and running shoes, can also affect the outcome of the MAF test. The bike setup and positioning, the pressure and wear on the tires, and any other factors that affect drag, such as clothing, will adversely affect the MAF test. You should note in your diary when you take the test using a different bike or bike setup or wearing more clothing, as well as other factors that may affect the test.

Running shoes may also affect the results of the MAF test. In general, shoes with more cushioning and more support and heavier shoes will slow your pace. Lighter shoes, including racing styles, generally result in faster MAF test times. (These issues are discussed in chapter 15.)

Stride length can also influence the MAF test. When a runner maintains a constant heart rate on a track, the optimal stride length may be determined by experimentation. If the stride length becomes inefficient, that is, if it's too short or too long, heart rate will rise. Studies show that variation in the stride length may significantly affect oxygen uptake. This is because increases and decreases in mechanical stress affect the running gait. Many runners may increase their stride length when they are fatigued. Oddly enough, this occurs when runners have a fever or a cold. Jogging or running at your most comfortable pace may correlate with the optimal stride length and the lowest heart rate.

Other equipment, such as treadmills, stationary bikes, step machines, and other devices can be used for the MAF test, but their results are not comparable to the results obtained using other equipment or test locations. For example, the treadmill MAF test is not comparable to running on a track, and a stationary bike test is not comparable to a test taken while riding a bike on a course on the road. Equipment maintenance may also affect the MAF test: poorly lubricated gears, improperly aligned wheels, or other structural inadequacies may adversely affect the MAF test.

In addition, a variety of health problems will worsen the MAF test time. These include fever, cold and flu, allergies, anemia, and other problems. More importantly, a MAF test result that is unexpectedly poor may be an indicator of an oncoming illness.

SOME FACTORS THAT AFFECT THE MAF TEST

FACTOR	EFFECT ON MAF TEST
Running track	
All-weather	improves
Dirt, grass, cinder	worsens
Indoor	improves
400-meter	improves
200-meter	worsens
Bike or skate	
Velodrome	improves
Smooth road	improves
Rough road	worsens
Hilly terrain	worsens
Weather	
Wind	worsens
Rain or snow	worsens
Humidity	worsens
Low barometric pressure	worsens
Very high or very low temperature	worsens
Altitude	
Higher	worsens
Lower	improves

MAF Test and Competition

I have long observed a relationship in competitive endurance runners between their MAF test results and their competitive times. I observed this relationship by analyzing data from several hundred MAF times and race results of healthy and fit runners competing in races between 5K and 10K over a five-year period. For example, a runner with a MAF test time of 8 minutes per mile should complete an average 5K race in just over 20 minutes, averaging about 6 minutes, 30 seconds per mile. This relationship can be considered one between maximum aerobic function (8 minutes per mile) and maximum anaerobic function (6 minutes, 30 seconds per mile). The chart below compares first-mile MAF test times with 5K average mile times for road races in healthy and fit athletes.

MAF AND PERFORMANCE

MAF (MIN. PER MILE)	5K RACE PACE	5K TIME
10:00	7:30	23:18
9:00	7:00	21:45
8:30	6:45	20:58
8:00	6:30	20:12
7:30	6:00	18:38
7:00	5:30	17:05
6:30	5:15	16:19
6:00	5:00	15:32

If your results don't match these expected results, the possibility of a structural, chemical, or mental *imbalance* should be considered. Take, for example, a runner with a MAF test time of 9 minutes per mile who runs a 5K race in 19 minutes, averaging just over 6 minutes per mile. This MAF test time of 9 minutes is *expected* to produce an average 5K race time of about 21 minutes, 45 seconds, or an average of about 7 minutes per mile. Instead, this athlete averages nearly a minute faster than expected. While this may appear to be a positive result, it is attained at the expense of some significant stress. This imbalance is not an uncommon one; such an imbalance often precedes a structural, chemical, or mental injury and typically represents an overtraining state.

Similarly, a runner whose first-mile MAF test time is 6 minutes 30 seconds is expected to finish a 5K race in 16 minutes 19 seconds. An actual time of 18 minutes would signal some imbalance. Perhaps the runner has some structural, chemical, or mental/emotional stress. A number of muscle imbalances could cause the slower time, or the problem might be nutritional (low nutrient intake), disturbing energy production. Or perhaps the runner was not mentally capable of "pushing" his or her body to its maximum potential.

The same type of data have not been collected for sports such as cycling or triathlon, since these races are too variable. But it can be assumed that the same relationships exist in cycling, triathlons, swimming, and even in sports such as tennis, basketball, hockey, and those that involve endurance. Improvement in performance almost always accompanies improvement in the MAF test results.

The use of a heart monitor can help you take the guesswork out of your exercise program. By glancing at your wrist watch, you can make sure that you don't exceed your maximum aerobic heart rate, assuring that you develop your fat-burning aerobic system.

More importantly, the MAF test can help plot your progress and warn you of any regression in your program. In addition, this test can help you prevent overtraining and injuries.

8

Warming Up, Cooling Down, and Stretching

When most people think of warming up before a workout, they think of stretching. However, not only does stretching not "warm" your body and prepare it for exercise, but it can be harmful. An active warm-up can more properly prepare you for an effective workout. Recovering from that workout with a proper cooldown can be just as important as preparing for it.

Warming Up

A proper warm-up prepares the body for activity and is an integral part of *every* workout and competition. The warm-up can reduce the muscle soreness associated with exercise, especially in persons just beginning an exercise program. In addition, a proper warm-up can reduce the risk of injury. Studies show that warmed-up muscles resist injury far better than muscles that are not warmed.

Too little or no warm-up can also cause an abnormal ECG, myocardial ischemia, and a poor blood-pressure response following exercise even in healthy, fit individuals. (Blood pressure should increase slightly at the onset of exercise, thereby helping to bring needed blood to muscles.) Cardiac patients in particular require a proper warm-up to reduce the heart's workload and oxygen requirements and to provide adequate coronary blood flow to the heart itself before exercise.

A proper warm-up consists of slowly elevating the heart rate through any aerobic or endurance activity. This may include walking (perhaps the best way to warm up), jogging, biking, step machines, swimming, or other similar activities. This type of warm-up, referred to as an *active* warm-up, should be performed before any exercise or competition, aerobic or anaerobic. The heart rate is only slightly elevated at the onset of the warm-up and continues to rise until the training heart rate is achieved at the end of the warm-up process (see below).

A runner may warm up by jogging slowly or, in some cases, walking. A golfer also may walk or jog if he or she is in good aerobic condition. An active warm-up will take at least 12 to 15 minutes, based on the duration of the total workout and how the athlete feels. Workouts lasting more than about 90 minutes require a longer warm-up. Athletes must learn to recognize when their body is prepared for more intense activity; most individuals experience this readiness as a looseness. Their gait becomes fluid, and they feel warmer.

One of the significant benefits of an active warm-up is the elevation of body temperature—the warming of the body. This warming of the body serves a number of important functions:

- *It improves the function or the utilization of oxygen in the hemoglobin (blood components) and myoglobin (muscle components).*

- *It makes energy production more efficient.*

- *It increases blood flow to working muscles.*

- *It produces greater mechanical efficiency of muscles, ligaments, tendons, and joints.*

- It improves the function of the nervous system.

- It improves the circulation of fatty acids (useful for energy in aerobic muscle fibers).

- It increases lung capacity, so that more air can be taken in and more carbon dioxide removed.

- It increases flexibility and improves your range of motion.

In some exercise or sports an *isolated* warm-up may consist of a modified version of the activity to come, usually performed after the active warm-up. For example, following a 20-minute easy walk a golfer initially makes easy, short swings with the club and gradually increases the range of motion, eventually making a normal stroke. A basketball player may following a 30-minute jog with easy tossing and dribbling the ball and work up to passing and shooting it farther, harder, and faster.

A heart monitor can greatly aid the athlete in the warm-up process by showing heart-rate progression as previously described. Athletes can easily observe their heart rate and avoid a too rapid or occasionally too leisurely elevation in heart rate. For example, an individual who begins warming up by jogging at a heart rate of 60 bpm will see his or her heart rate gradually increase to 80, 100, and higher. After 15 minutes the maximum aerobic heart rate is achieved, and training intensity may be maintained.

If a longer workout is planned, a warm-up of increased duration is recommended.

Cooling Down

Cooling down, also called "active recovery" or "warming down," is recommended after all workouts and most competitions. This involves diminishing the level of exercise intensity while the heart rate is reduced. This active recovery is very different from *passive recovery*, which involves complete rest following a workout, reserved for those persons who are completely exhausted following competition.

A proper cooldown performs some very important functions:

- *It makes more oxygen available to the muscles by increasing circulation through the muscle fibers.*

- *It rapidly removes blood lactate and other by-products of exercise.*

- *During intermittent sports such as basketball, football, and track and field competition, in which exercise is always starting and stopping, active recovery from one bout of activity results in more anaerobic power during the next bout.*

- *It helps prevent blood from pooling in the extremities, particularly the legs, which can result in dizziness, faintness, or even fainting.*

The Right Rate

Patty is a distance runner with an aerobic training heart rate of 155 bpm. She begins her long, 90-minute run with a resting heart rate of 58 bpm. A slow jog elevates that rate to 70 bpm, and as she increases her speed, her heart rate matches the faster pace. After about 8 minutes Patty's heart rate is 105 bpm, and after about 12 minutes it is 120 bpm. She begins to feel loose, and her stride is comfortable. At 16 minutes her heart rate is 140 bpm. It increases to about 150 bpm at 20 minutes, and she starts to feel good. Patty reaches her maximum training heart rate of 155 bpm after about 24 minutes, and she maintains that rate, adjusting her pace on hills, 70 minutes into the run. At 70 minutes she begins to slow her pace and lower her heart rate. At 75 minutes her heart rate is 135; it gradually decreases until at 85 minutes she is running at a heart rate of under 100 bpm. At the end of her run Patty's heart rate is 85, and she walks for 5 minutes to bring it down to about 80 bpm. Patty feels that she could almost perform the same workout again without undue stress.

Most importantly, the ability to perform an efficient cooldown is dependent on the functioning of the aerobic muscle fibers. It is important, therefore, to develop a good aerobic system.

Awareness of your heart rate can also assist you in cooling down. In general, you should slowly reduce your heart rate until it is close to your starting rate; it is not necessary, nor is it usually possible, to reduce your heart rate to its pretraining level. Similar to a warm-up, an extended workout is best completed with a longer active-recovery period.

Note that the warm-up and recovery are considered *part of the workout*. For example, a 60-minute workout *includes* a 15-minute warm-up and a 15-minute recovery. This leaves 30 minutes for training at the maximum aerobic heart rate (or other intensities as planned).

Active Warm-Up and Recovery in Competition

A proper warm-up is vital before competition, and some athletes find that their warm-up lasts longer than their actual event. A 5K race may last less than 20 minutes, for example, but a typical runner with a good aerobic system and competitive experience may take 30 to 45 minutes or longer to warm up. Shorter warm-ups that include walking may be used before considerably longer events, such as marathons or Ironman triathlons.

Anyone who competes in anaerobic events may benefit from proper warm-ups and recovery periods. For example, a football player who is in and out of the game and a sprinter who must compete in several heats to qualify for the finals both need a good initial warm-up consisting of 20 to 30 minutes of increasingly intense activity that mimics their event. During the actual competition, periods of activity should be followed by relatively brief active-recovery periods, and the cycle should be repeated until the game or event is over. Ideally, another period of active recovery should follow the last bout of activity.

As emphasized, a good warm-up is dependent on a highly developed aerobic system. If an athlete's heart rate soars to 180 bpm during an easy warm-up, he or she clearly should not be performing that activity before a workout or competition, as it may cause fatigue or even injury. This is usually an indication that the athlete's aerobic system is not well developed.

Stretching

The ongoing debate over the usefulness of stretching is complex, controversial, and inconclusive. In my opinion, based on treating many types of athletes, including beginners, most exercisers don't need to stretch if they properly warm up and cool down. Only athletes who require a greater than normal range of motion, such as dancers and track-and-field athletes, may need to stretch. In addition, it's clear to me, and it has been observed by many other professionals as well, that people who stretch experience more injuries than people who do not stretch.

Most athletes regard stretching and the resultant increase in range of motion (ROM) as a form of injury prevention. However, scientific/medical studies on the preventive effect of stretching are scarce and contradictory. The relationship between flexibility

Even for Golf

John plays golf several times per week. He begins with 20 minutes of easy walking, followed by 10 minutes at a faster pace. Then, with a four iron, he begins making short, effortless practice swings, taking 10 minutes to work up to a full swing with a wood club. John hits balls on the practice range for another 10 to 15 minutes. If he feels that his body still isn't warm enough, he continues to practice on the driving range.

The Maffetone Method

derived from stretching and freedom from injury has not been established. And some studies plainly demonstrate that *increased flexibility produces more injuries.*

The controversy that surrounds stretching results in part from the difference between ballistic and static stretching, the two most common types of stretching. Other types of stretching are variations of these two types.

Ballistic stretching involves repetitive, bouncing movements that use the body's momentum to repeatedly stretch a joint to or beyond ROM extremes. This may be the most harmful type of stretching, but it is the most common, possibly because most people are in a hurry to begin their workout. Ballistic stretching may activate the stretch reflex and actually *increase tension* and the risk for micro-tears in the muscle.

Static stretching involves very slowly stretching the muscle to a point of slight discomfort (not burning or pain) and then holding it for up to 30 seconds. Each muscle group is sequentially stretched three to four times, and it is essential that the routine not be rushed. Static stretching may be either active or passive. *Active static stretching* contracts the opposite (antagonist) muscle. *Passive static stretching* typically requires force by another person (or body part) to move a body segment to the end of, or beyond, its range of motion.

Performed properly, static stretching relaxes the muscle. However, the time commitment is substantial. Considering the risks of stretching and the fact that a proper warm-up provides significant increases in flexibility, your time may best be spent warming up and cooling down.

9

The Aerobic
Deficiency Syndrome

*Most Americans fall into one of the follow-
ing categories: they exercise too little or not
at all, are not naturally active, and are
aerobically deficient; or they overexercise
(overtrain) or are excessively stressed. Some
people fall into both categories. Either one
can result in poor aerobic function.*

Poor aerobic function can lead to a variety of common complaints that can have a significant negative impact on the quality of
your life. This chapter provides a checklist of signs and symptoms
to help you determine whether you suffer from the aerobic deficiency syndrome (ADS).

Quantity versus Quality of Life

We often hear that our life expectancy continues to rise, as if it is an
indication of how well our health care system is working. Without
a doubt, we're living longer. But our quality of life isn't necessarily

high. In the United States, the period of dysfunction at the end of our life span—the period when we are unable to care for ourselves or recognize others and even ourselves—averages 12 years. That means that we spend well over a decade of our life "living" a slow death. We all know someone in this state—a parent, grandparent, or neighbor—and we all fear this end stage of our lives. But there's really a lot we can do to avert such a tragic ending.

Much of the dysfunction that accompanies these last 12 years of our life begins with very subtle signs and symptoms many years earlier. These clues, some of which are discussed below, should serve as indications that something is wrong and appropriate action must be taken. I'm horrified at how poorly some people care for themselves. Then when they get older and dysfunctional, they want a magic pill to make them functional again. There's no magic pill, but there's something almost as good: good aerobic function.

The time to act is now. One major imbalance that lowers our quality of life now is ADS. And if it becomes chronic, it can have a devastating effect on us later in life. Heart disease, diabetes, hypertension, stroke, and certain cancers are among the many problems that some of us face unless we make our body more functional starting now.

ADS

Simply put, ADS is usually the result of an imbalance between aerobic and anaerobic function, specifically low aerobic and comparatively high anaerobic function. In addition, adrenal dysfunction is a common associated factor, most often resulting from excessive physical, chemical, or mental stress.

People often complain of a variety of seemingly unrelated problems that are common to ADS. These include the signs and symptoms listed below. It should be noted that any of these problems could have other causes. You'll see that many are similar to adrenal dysfunction. That's because ADS and adrenal problems often occur together.

In the list below check the problems that pertain to you. If you check two of these problems, you may be starting to lose your aerobic function; if you check three, you may already be aerobically deficient; and if you check four or more, it's likely that you have ADS, and it may be chronic.

1. **Fatigue.** This may be the most common complaint of the average person. It may be fatigue in the morning (difficulty getting out of bed), in the afternoon (a very low period in the mid-afternoon), or all day. It may be physical fatigue or mental fatigue, the latter impairing your concentration and your ability to focus on your work. In extreme cases exhaustion is the word that best describes the feeling. Fatigue, or sleepiness, following meals may be related to excess carbohydrates in your diet (see chapter 20).

2. **Blood sugar stress.** This problem is more difficult to evaluate without blood tests, but the symptoms include frequent hunger, feeling shaky if meals are delayed or missed, and cravings for sweets or caffeine. This problem is often associated with a carbohydrate intolerance, the inability to eat a high-carbohydrate diet without excess fat storage, and the accompanying blood sugar stress. Most individuals with this problem are following a diet high in carbohydrates and low in fat.

3. **Increased body fat.** Some people eat a diet containing the right number of calories and not too high in fats and exercise regularly but still gain weight and body fat. This stored body fat can find its way to any area—hips, abdomen, arms, even the arteries. Where the body stores it may be mostly a matter of genetics, and you can't "spot reduce." More upper body fat (especially in the abdomen) may indicate that you're eating a diet that is too high in carbohydrates, much of which turns to fat and is stored; bread, sweets, cereals, potatoes, and other carbohydrates may be more of a problem than dietary fat (see chapter 20).

4. **Structural injuries.** Specific injuries are common and may be due to the lack of aerobic muscle support around your joints. The lower back, knee, ankle, and foot are the most vulnerable areas of structural injury in ADS. These problems

may be recurrent; sometimes the injury recurs at the same site, and other times it seems to "travel" from one area to another. This often prevents regular exercise, creating a vicious cycle. Many of these physical problems can be resolved if you can break the cycle: find a workout that won't aggravate your injury, such as swimming, cycling, or water aerobics. Remember, it doesn't take much effort to build a good aerobic system.

5. **Menstrual and menopausal symptoms.** These are two common problems in women, often associated with ADS and with an imbalance in adrenal hormones, specifically, high levels of cortisol and low levels of DHEA. In addition, amenorrhea (the cessation of the menstrual period) is often associated with excess exercise and overtraining (see chapter 10).

6. **Reduced endurance.** This is most evident in an inability to continue to perform well all day long. For the competitive athlete, longer workouts become more difficult and competitive skills lessen. And the MAF test, perhaps one of the best methods of evaluating aerobic function, shows a decline in performance.

7. **Mental and emotional stress.** This condition may include feelings of depression, anxiety or a clinical depression being the most common symptoms. This problem may come and go, may come at only certain times of the month, or may be constant.

8. **Insomnia.** In the type of sleep disturbance associated with ADS, it's easy to fall asleep (often because you're so tired), but then you wake in the middle of the night and have a difficult time getting back to sleep. You're seemingly full of energy and wonder why you don't have that much energy during the day. Many people say the need to urinate awakens them, but more often you wake first, and the need to go to the bathroom is secondary.

9. **Poor circulation.** Because there is so much circulation in aerobic muscle fibers, poor aerobic capacity usually results in a lesser number of functional blood vessels. This reduces the

amount of circulation. The classic symptoms include cold hands and feet and sometimes being cold all over. Varicose veins and hemorrhoids may also accompany this problem.

10. **Sexual dysfunction.** *Sexual dysfunction usually takes the form of a reduced sex drive. It's normal to have a desire for sex throughout your life, not just when you're in your twenties. When you're aerobically deficient, you're too tired in the evening and the hormones (those that fuel the desire for sex, such as testosterone) are low. Sexual dysfunction is a frequent cause of stress, which then further aggravates the problem.*

Correcting ADS

The good news is that ADS can be remedied. In most cases you can correct the condition yourself. Recovery first involves evaluating your life. Ask yourself these three simple questions:

- *Am I building my aerobic system through proper exercise?*

- *Have I overdeveloped my anaerobic system with exercise?*

- *Am I overstressed?*

Making the appropriate changes as described in this book is often all it takes to correct the aerobic deficiency syndrome. However, diet and nutrition are often part of the problem and the correction (see the brief discussion in chapter 20).

In some cases it's necessary to seek assistance from a professional. However, find a professional who is familiar with functional problems, which is the gray area, rather than one who is aware of only the two ends of the full spectrum—optimal health at one end and disease at the other.

10

The Overtraining Syndrome

Many people who exercise go too far. They place undue stress on their physical, chemical, and mental body, a common condition known as overtraining. It is nearly identical to other over-stress conditions and can be corrected in the same way: by balancing the aerobic and anaerobic systems. In a real sense, overtraining is a common obsession that has become a tradition.

There is no standard definition of overtraining; it traditionally has been described as diminished performance resulting from an increase in training volume and/or intensity. The most practical definition is discussed in chapter 1: overtraining occurs when there is an imbalance in the equation

training = workout + rest

This may result from an excessive number or intensity of workouts, lack of recovery, or a combination of both. This problem has multiple causes and is best referred to as the *overtraining syndrome*. It is associated with nervous system, hormonal (adrenal dysfunction in particular), and nutritional and dietary deficiencies.

The more common symptoms of the overtraining syndrome include poor performance, structural injury, fatigue, recurrent infections, and altered mood states. The diminished performance associated with overtraining occurs not only in athletic competition but in everyday activities—learning, thinking, physical work, or any other daily activity.

Evaluating the overtraining syndrome in its earliest stages is crucial if further regression is to be prevented. The MAF test may be the most effective way to do this. In addition, if you are aerobically deficient and exercising regularly, you may be overtrained without knowing it. Some people who don't appear to be overexercising during individual sessions are surprised to find that they are really overtrained. Remember, this condition occurs not only in persons who work out too hard but also in persons who exercise too much and especially in persons who do not allow enough time for recovery. Even a moderate exercise schedule accompanied by other kinds of stress can lead to overtraining.

Three Stages of Overtraining

Overtraining has three stages, and it is not always clear where one stage ends and the next begins. The first is not well defined in the medical literature, but the other two are. The three stages are

1. *Functional overtraining*

2. *Sympathetic overtraining*

3. *Parasympathetic overtraining*

Stage 1

Stage 1 is the stage in which the onset of overtraining may be detected. For a professional who has observed this condition for many years, it's relatively easy to determine functional overtraining in most people. What is most difficult, however, is for the individual to determine that he or she is functionally overtrained.

Performing the MAF test regularly is one way to objectively

check for this stage of overtraining. You will see an abnormal plateau or regression in your progress. In addition, if you are exercising regularly, you'll find that two or more of the signs or symptoms of ADS exist. An important and interesting observation about overtraining in competitive athletes is that the first stage *sometimes* is accompanied by a sudden and dramatic *improvement* in competitive performance that may convince the athlete that all is going well. Decreased performance levels always follow but sometimes not until the second or third stage of overtraining.

Stage 1 overtraining may be synonymous with what is called *overreaching*, which has been shown to temporarily boost performance but often turns into overtraining. Overreaching is exercising slightly beyond your normal capability as a means of progressing. However, there is a fine line between healthful overreaching and the kind of overreaching that you can't recover from.

Stage 2

Stage 2 overtraining is also called *sympathetic overtraining* because of the stress it places on the sympathetic nervous system. It begins following the end of stage 1 and becomes more obvious, in a sense revving up your nervous system. This is typically reflected in a higher resting heart rate, more easily observed in the morning, general restlessness and hyperexcitability, and a clear *regression* in MAF test results. Stage 2 is more common in people who train with speed or high intensity, power, or increased frequency and in people with contributing lifestyle stress. A combination of these factors is more typical.

Stage 2 is also associated with adrenal dysfunction and ADS. This stage is often characterized by the imbalance between cortisol and DHEA—too much cortisol and too little DHEA. Generally, high cortisol levels have a catabolic effect on the system, much like that produced by exhaustive, prolonged training, leading to a tearing down of the body. Cortisol measurement may be a valuable laboratory test. However, an experienced practitioner can accurately predict this problem if the patient has furnished a complete history. Stage 2 overtraining can also adversely affect the keen awareness and fine hand-to-eye coordination required in sports such as golf, racquet sports, and basketball.

Low testosterone levels, secondary to reduced levels of DHEA, may also be a good laboratory test to indicate overtraining. Testosterone creates significant problems for athletes because it's important for muscle recovery. Taking DHEA, however, is not always the best remedy, as this would amount to treating the symptoms and not the cause. DHEA supplements may temporarily relieve some symptoms, but the end result may be other, more chronic aerobic, adrenal, and overtraining problems that are even more difficult to correct.

When stage 2 overtraining continues, it may lead to the third stage of overtraining.

Stage 3

Stage 3 overtraining is referred to as *parasympathetic overtraining* because it affects the parasympathetic part of the nervous system. It is accompanied by a relative *decreased* resting heart rate, a reduced or absent desire to compete, and more commonly, a reduced desire for working out. Depression and, most notably, exhaustion are also common. The MAF test has usually significantly regressed and plateaued at a low level. Some persons mistakenly interpret the low resting heart rate that accompanies this condition as a good sign.

Any of the other signs and symptoms of overtraining, such as ADS and adrenal dysfunction, may accompany this third stage. Individuals in this stage of overtraining often suffer from a multitude of complaints. Sometimes their physicians refer these persons to other professionals for psychological or psychiatric help because no clear disease state can be found.

Menstrual Problems and Overtraining

Menstrual dysfunction is frequently associated with overtraining, especially in women and girls who regularly perform high-intensity exercise. Overtraining may produce such menstrual abnormalities as amenorrhea (the absence of a menstrual period), oligomenorrhoea (a menstrual cycle between 35 and 90 days), and delayed menarche (the onset of menstruation) in girls. These problems may begin in the early years. For example, studies of female athletes show that only 20 percent of the gymnasts (13.3 years of age on average) and 40 percent of the runners (13.6 years on average) had started menstruating, compared with 95 percent of noncompetitive girls of a similar age.

In some cases of amenorrhea, disordered eating (especially in individuals following a low-calorie and/or low-fat diet) accompanies overtraining. Persons suffering from this kind of amenorrhea often have an excessively low body weight and excessively low body fat (especially fat around the hips, buttocks, and thighs) and eat a vegetarian diet. Increased consumption of carbohydrates, especially sweets, or a low-fat diet may aggravate the problem.

One of the most significant problems associated with amenorrhea is bone loss. This results from prolonged periods of low estrogen and progesterone levels, which increase the risk of reduced bone density, stress fractures, muscle soreness, and physical fatigue. Bone loss is most common in the spine, wrists, and feet. These imbalances can lead to skeletal problems—scoliosis in the early years, osteoporosis later in life. (It should be noted that in boys and men reduced testosterone can also cause bone loss.)

Correction of Overtraining

The remedy for overtraining depends on the individual's needs. Correction typically includes restructuring the training schedule and modifying lifestyle factors related to stress. Here are some suggestions for a three- to six-month period:

- *Decrease the total time of each exercise session by 50 percent, or more if necessary.*

- *Immediately cease all anaerobic training, including weight lifting and competition.*

- *Walking is helpful. Don't underestimate the therapeutic benefits of walking: it gently stimulates circulation and aerobic*

muscle fiber activity, is mentally beneficial (much like medi-
tation), and can help redevelop the aerobic system—the
first phase of retraining.

- *Retraining, that is, building the aerobic base, should last*
  three to six months and should not include any anaerobic
  training or competition.

In addition, make the stress list discussed in chapter 2, evaluate yourself for ADS and adrenal dysfunction, and make all the necessary improvements.

Most people can recover from the overtraining syndrome. Recovery from stage 1 overtraining can typically be accomplished within three to four months. Recovery from stage 2 overtraining may take at least six months. And for those persons who are chronically overtrained, or can be categorized as being in the third stage of overtraining, recovery can take a year or longer. These individuals may recover faster if they work with a professional, so they can tailor the recovery program to their needs.

Overtraining is a serious condition. Fortunately, it is relatively easy to prevent, not usually difficult to evaluate when you are honest with yourself, and in most cases correctable in a reasonable time frame. However, it is first necessary for the individual to recognize the problem and be willing to take the time to remedy it. By doing so, he or she can eliminate a significant health and fitness imbalance and not only restore but also improve the functioning of his or her body.

Part 2

INDIVIDUALIZING YOUR PROGRAM

11

A New Beginning: Starting Your Program

> Perhaps the most important recommendation for anyone beginning an exercise program is this: keep it simple. It should not be complicated, expensive, tiring, or otherwise unpleasant. Chances are that if it's simple it will be fun—and you'll begin reaping great benefits after your very first workout.

Whether you're 14 or 104, it's never too early or too late to start exercising. The benefits will begin the very first day. The question is, where do you begin? That's really a question only you can answer. Some individuals will need assistance from a professional, who can help to assure that they will have no risks. This chapter gives you some healthful and realistic ideas about how to begin an exercise program.

Many people truly want to exercise. They are aware of the benefits, and in many cases their doctor has told them to start exercising. There are several reasons why people never begin. One reason is their perception of what it means to work out. We see images (on TV and in magazine or newspaper ads) of people straining to the point of collapse, and think, "I don't want to do that!" We see those with "abs of steel" and wonder, "How could I get there?" When we pass a runner on the road, what we usually see is not a joyful expression but rather a pained one.

Another common reason why people never start a program is that they're never told what to do. Most people who are not completely turned off by the images they see don't have a clue where to begin. In addition, some people have a friend, family member, or acquaintance who has been injured or overtrained through exercise abuse.

Start Simply

James was becoming more overweight, not a good sign considering a family history of diabetes and heart disease. Following a recent physical exam, his doctor correctly encouraged James to exercise, explaining the benefits and statistics. James agreed with the whole idea. He toured the local gym, thinking that it would be the most convenient approach, but was discouraged by what he saw—the muscular bodies and mirrors, hard-working young athletes. He peeked in at the aerobics class, which included a number of men, but they were working out at such a frantic pace, the music was so loud, that it nearly made him fatigued. The following week, James went to look at some exercise equipment so that he could work out at home. He changed his mind after he tried to lift one of the dumbbells the salesperson tried to sell him. After several weeks James lost interest in exercise. Several months later, feeling even worse, he came to my clinic. He agreed to a simple program of walking 30 minutes each day during his lunch break, but he wondered how that would help. After two months James was feeling so good that several of his coworkers remarked on how good he looked and began walking with him.

The Maffetone Method

Walking

Of all the types of exercise, walking is the one I recommend most often for those just starting. (It's also a workout I've given to professional athletes because of its great health benefits.) Walking is the safest workout: the intensity level usually remains low, yet the benefits are great. Walking burns a higher percentage of fat (not necessarily more fat) than most other activities and better programs your body to burn more fat throughout the day (not just during your workout) because of its low intensity.

Walking very effectively develops the small aerobic muscle fibers. These are the ones that may not be stimulated in higher-intensity workouts, especially anaerobic training. Walking also improves blood circulation and lymph drainage (a part of the body's waste-removal system).

Walking is one of the best ways to get started on an exercise program because it's simple, inexpensive, and provides a low-stress workout that is not easily overdone. Walkers generally have little difficulty keeping their heart rate from getting too high, though there are exceptions. If walking has a disadvantage, it's that it doesn't raise your heart rate high enough, or near your maximum aerobic heart rate. However, this isn't absolutely necessary at the beginning of an exercise program. The mechanics of walking result in less gravity stress than you would experience jogging or running but enough to strengthen your bones and improve your aerobic system.

When I say walking, I'm not referring to power walking, race walking, or carrying weights while you walk—just an easy walk. If inactive people knew how easy it was to get great benefits from exercise by easy walking, more of them would surely do it. More people are at risk for coronary heart disease because they don't get this kind of exercise than are at risk because of any other factors, and not doing easy walking is also an independent risk factor for coronary heart disease, doubling the risk. Inactivity puts one at almost as great a risk for coronary heart disease as cigarette smoking and hypertension.

Here are some benefits of easy walking:

- *It increases life expectancy.*

- *It helps older adults maintain their functional independence, an important concern for society. Currently, the average number of nonfunctional years in our elderly population is about 12. That's a dozen years at the end of their life span when they are unable to care for themselves, be productive, or just enjoy life.*

- *By improving the balance of fats in the blood, clotting, and individuals' ability to more efficiently regulate blood sugar, it can help prevent and manage coronary heart disease, the leading cause of death in the United States, as well as hypertension, diabetes, osteoporosis, and depression.*

- *It is associated with a lower incidence of colon cancer, stroke, and lower-back injury.*

All this and more can be accomplished with easy aerobic exercise. How easy? The equivalent of a sustained 30-minute walk four times a week. Unfortunately, only 12 percent of Americans are even this active on a daily basis, and only 22 percent exercise this much five times per week.

Children and Exercise

More serious than the above statistics is that only 36 percent of U.S. children in grades 1 through 12 have physical education daily. We know that physical activity improves academic achievement and has a positive effect on the health and well-being of children. The American Academy of Pediatrics and the American College of Sports Medicine have lobbied to increase the time schools devote to physical education. The U.S. Congress passed a resolution encouraging state and local educational agencies to require schools to do just that; unfortunately, most states haven't complied. And students who do take gym class are physically active a mere 27 percent of the time. Twenty-six percent of the time is spent on instruction, an important feature of physical education, but almost half of the time is wasted: 25 percent is spent waiting, and 22 percent is spent on administrative tasks.

The clear answer to this problem is for parents to get just as involved in their children's physical education as they are in their academic education. The best way to influence children, of course, is through example. A child who sees Mom and Dad going for daily walks will be more interested in participating in sports activities. The whole family can be physically active together. It's also not difficult to push a stroller as you take your walk, which is good for both parent and child.

Other Activities

Although walking is by far the best way to start a program, some would prefer other options. Other activities can be just as effective, but more care is needed because they involve a greater potential for overdoing it—overtraining—than walking. Here are some additional ways to start your exercise program:

▶ *Stationary bikes. There are many types available. Keep it simple. You should be able to adjust the tension and the seat height, and the bike should be comfortable. You should set the tension at the lowest level. You just need to go through the motions in the beginning. You should also adjust the seat to a height that is right for your body size. When sitting on the bike, place your feet on the pedals. When the pedal is at its lowest point, your knee should be only very slightly bent. This reduces potential mechanical stress on your ankles, knees, hips, and pelvis. It's ideal to have someone knowledgeable help you with these adjustments. If the bike is not comfortable, don't use it.*

▶ *Aerobic dance. Any type of dancing—including ballroom dancing—can be very good for those starting a workout program. However, if you're with a group of experienced dancers, or dancers who are already in good shape, don't try to keep up. If you can't go at your own pace, avoid the class until you're in better shape. You could start at home by yourself or with a friend whose condition is comparable to your own.*

▶ **Treadmills.** *The use of a motorized treadmill is nearly as good as walking outdoors. There is no need to elevate the surface (if the treadmill has that option) for the first couple of months. However, you should avoid treadmills that are not motorized, which force you to power the tread yourself. This typically results in a much higher heart rate and an anaerobic workout.*

These approaches may be slightly more risky than walking. Using a heart rate monitor could be a great help in reducing potential risk by making sure you work out at or below your proper heart rate level.

Exercises to Avoid

There are several types of workouts that are not recommended for individuals just beginning a program. Usually these routines raise the heart rate too much or require more skill and exertion than most people wish.

▶ **Skipping rope.** *Most beginners are not able to skip rope for two reasons: first, it may take some time to develop the proper technique; and second, developing the technique generally rapidly elevates your heart rate. This means that you're doing an anaerobic workout, which often leads to exhaustion. Also, a location with a high enough ceiling and a floor you can jump on is sometimes difficult to find.*

▶ **Ab machines.** *These machines are so named because they exercise the abdominal muscles, or "abs." They are touted as a way to trim your belly. Unfortunately, they not only don't develop the aerobic system but also discourage most users in a short time. In addition, there's no such thing as "spot" reducing.*

▶ **Step machines.** There are a number of different types of steppers and stair machines on the market. They can be effective for the beginner if you're careful to watch your heart rate. However, they tend to work your muscles more than your metabolism, and fatigue tends to discourage many people.

▶ **Weights.** As discussed earlier, weight lifting, including weight machines, is anaerobic, and these workouts won't adequately build your aerobic system.

▶ **Rowing machines and rider machines.** On these devices you sit and either row or perform similar actions using your arms and legs. Although these machines provide a good workout for individuals who are in better shape, they generally are not appropriate for the beginner. They usually require more anaerobic activity and cause the heart rate to rise too high.

▶ **Ski machines.** Ski machines are another good idea for those in better shape, but they are too difficult for the average beginner and tend to increase the heart rate. Also, I've seen many injuries resulting from their use.

It's most important to find the method you feel most comfortable with and go with it. Walking is nearly fail-safe and inexpensive, and those who walk tend to maintain their program longer than those who do other exercises.

Your First Workout

The best time to start your program is now, after reading the remainder of this chapter. If necessary, be sure to consult with your doctor or professional. All that is required is for you to dress appropriately and wear comfortable footwear, preferably very flat sneakers or even barefoot. Let's use the example of walking, although if you're riding a stationary bike or dancing in your living room the same considerations apply.

Walk for a specified amount of time rather than distance. To start, 20–30 minutes may be a great workout. Don't let anyone tell you it's not long enough or that you need to walk fast. You don't. If you have any discomfort during this time, stop. If you're tired after 20–30 minutes, or if you have any discomfort, next time walk for only 10–15 minutes. There will be a length of time that makes you feel good, not tired or hurt. Even a 5-minute walk may be a good starting point.

After your workout you should feel as if you could do the same workout again. But don't. That's how it should feel. The next morning, you should not have any negative effects—you should not have discomfort such as painful joints or muscles. If you do, you may have worked out too long. Wait a day before working out again, and then diminish the time. It is normal to feel a very slight soreness or tenderness in your muscles. That's a normal part of their adaptation to working out. But it should not be uncomfortable or painful.

It may be best to walk by yourself. However, if you need more motivation, walking with a friend is a great idea. In areas where safety may be an issue, then walking with another person or a group may be safer. If you walk with others, be sure you're not moving at a faster pace than if you walked alone. It should not be a competitive workout.

When in doubt, go slower. It never hurts to work out easier, but working too hard can have adverse consequences.

Understand that after only one workout you're getting exercise benefits—you've increased circulation, stimulated more fat burning, exercised your heart, and benefited in other ways that will continue to make you healthier and more fit.

Once you get through the first day in good shape, and all is well the next day, continue with the same workout time. Here are some other important considerations for future progress:

▶ **Weekly routine.** *If you feel good after your walk, try walking on consecutive days. You should continue to feel good after each walk. If you can't walk three or four days in a row without tiring, walk two days and take one day off, then walk two days. Some persons will have no trouble walking four or five days in a row. Walking four to five days with a day or two off is a good starting point.*

▶ **Location.** *Walk anywhere that has a relatively smooth surface, such as blacktop, a dirt trail, or a school track. Shopping centers are sometimes good places (especially in the morning, before the stores open). Be sure that the place you walk is safe from traffic, bikers, dogs, and other potential dangers.*

▶ **Increasing your time.** *In the beginning, the most important aspect of your exercise program is finding the best starting time. Eventually you may wish to increase your workout time. If you start by exercising 20 minutes, after about a month you can increase to 30 minutes. Consider the same factors: if 30 minutes makes you tired or gives discomfort, it's too much. In that case try 25 minutes.*

▶ **Increasing your pace.** *In a short time you'll be burning more fat, your aerobic muscle fibers will be developing, and you'll be able to do more (such as walk faster) with the same effort (i.e., the same heart rate). As a result, your pace will quicken naturally. But just because walking becomes easier, don't push yourself. More is not necessarily better. Rather than increase your pace, gradually increase your total workout time.*

▶ **Progressing.** *Gradually increase your workout time to 45 minutes. This may take you a couple of months or even a year. There's no rush. However, if 30 minutes is comfortable, and all you want to do or have time to do, you'll still get good aerobic benefits. Progressing to 45 minutes will just provide more benefits and enable you to build your aerobic system more quickly.*

12

Modifying Your Program

You've been working out for a while, perhaps you belong to a health club, and sometimes you even work out at home. But you're often fatigued, your body fat seems too high, and injuries seem to come out of nowhere. Or perhaps you have lags in your routine—you exercise for a few days or a couple of weeks and then miss the next few weeks. Or you may jump from program to program, hoping to find the right one. You may have no self-motivation, no good feelings from working out, and there seems to be no reason to exercise. But your body wants exercise, and needs it, and you need answers.

If you can't answer "yes" to all the questions in the accompanying box, you may need to modify your program. The more "no" answers, the more you need to change. That's because a workout program that matches your particular needs results in

- *measurable progress*
- *increased energy*
- *correction and prevention of injury*
- *increased fat burning*
- *fun—feeling good during and after your workout*

In all likelihood, you're already working out to some degree, albeit inconsistently or otherwise ineffectively. You're committed to making it part of your lifestyle. Now it's time for a tune-up. There are four factors that can help modify your current program: goals, equipment, aerobic base, and direction and measurement.

Is Your Workout Working?

Is your program really giving you what you want, or does it only frustrate you? Here are some questions that may help you decide whether your workout plan is working for you or against you.

1. *Have you been able to measure your exercise progress?*
2. *Is your energy good from the time you wake up until you go to bed?*
3. *Are you free from injuries, even seemingly little aches and pains?*
4. *Is your body fat at a controllable level?*
5. *Do you look forward to working out (i.e., is it fun)?*
6. *Do you feel good after your workout?*

Goals

Before doing anything about your program, sit down—by yourself or with a trainer or professional who understands you and exercise—and look at the big picture. Ask yourself these three important questions:

- *What was my health and fitness level before I started my program (better, worse, or the same)?*
- *What is my health and fitness level now (better, worse, or the same)?*

- *What do I want my health and fitness level to be in the future, compared with what it is today (better, worse, or the same)?*

It's important to understand your own health and fitness history. If your level of health and fitness is no better now, or even worse, than it was before you began working out, it's obvious that something is not working. You may also have been able to assess this from the six questions at the beginning of the chapter.

Even more important is knowing where you're going—knowing what your exercise goals are. If you don't have any, it's important to formulate some, especially a primary one. Here are some things to consider when formulating your goals:

- **What is your primary goal?** *It's important to have a main focus. This may be somewhat general, such as getting into good shape, losing weight and body fat, or competing in a race. In reality, it's one big package. Even if you just want to get into better shape, you'll also burn more fat, lose weight, and be capable of competition. But you still should have a specific goal to focus on.*

- **Make your goals realistic, but don't be afraid to dream.** *If you're a hundred pounds overweight and your goal is to run a marathon (26 miles), that may be unrealistic for next month but not as a long-term goal. Or maybe now that you can walk without pain you realize that hiking the Appalachian Trail may be realistic—but perhaps only part of it for now. In order to formulate realistic goals, you need to be aware of any disabilities or other restrictions you may have, such as a heart problem or diabetes, which may limit your workout capability. Most people have few, if any, limitations. In determining whether your goals are realistic, you may need input from a professional.*

- **Review and focus on your primary goal on a regular basis.** *This will help you get out of bed to work out on cold, dark winter mornings. Losing focus could make you inconsistent or more clumsy and increase the likelihood that you'll lose your direction. If you lose your focus, you may get hooked into a friend's workout routine or be taken in by a magazine article* (typically a "no pain, no gain" one), ending up in an entirely different workout program from the one you planned.

- **Secondary goals may also be important, and the same rules apply.** These may include attaining a certain weight or clothing size, being able to maintain a workout schedule without injury, or reducing your blood pressure. Be careful about setting unrealistic or unnecessary goals here too. If your goal is to run a first marathon, that's enough of a goal. Adding a secondary goal of running it in less than four hours can be a stretch. Just completing a marathon is sufficient.

- **Review your goals regularly to determine whether you need to modify them.** For example, you may suddenly have to put in many hours of overtime at work. Becoming pregnant, moving to another part of the country, or other significant changes in your life would also require you to modify your goals. Sometimes the need is not so obvious. Perhaps you've lost interest in running a marathon but feel that you've made a commitment. If it's not going to be fun, don't do it.

It's especially important for you to write down your goals. The best place to do this is in a workout diary, discussed below.

Equipment

The most important piece of equipment is usually not thought of as equipment: your workout diary. It's an item that can help you work out better, but it is more of a mental apparatus than a physical apparatus. A diary can be as formal as a special book you write in after each workout or as informal as notes on a separate calendar. Whatever form your diary takes, use it only for recording your workouts; don't make it part of the family "to do" list or your business diary.

Your workout diary should include (1) your primary and secondary goals, (2) your basic workout strategies, and (3) your day-to-day workout activities.

1. *Your goals should be listed somewhere in your diary, apart from everything else. If you make changes or modifications, don't erase your previous goals, but write in the modifications. This will ultimately give you a record of your goalmaking patterns. Did you change your goals because they're unrealistic? Or do you have too little confidence in your ability to attain your original goals and then replace them with goals that are too conservative?*

2. *Your basic workout strategies include your training heart rate for aerobic workouts, the ongoing results of your MAF tests, and the specific workout program you make for yourself. You may also wish to include the specific exercise equipment you use, the shoes you wear, and any other "standard" items or routines.*

3. *Most of your diary will consist of accounts of your individual workouts. Include any and all information regarding each workout. This varies greatly from person to person. You should include at least the following items:*
   - *Total workout time*
   - *Type of workout (e.g., stationary bike, jog on park trail, etc.)*
   - *Any deviation from the basic rules (e.g., "forgot to cool down properly" or "ran too fast")*
   - *Time of day*
   - *How you felt before, during, and after. This should include your general feeling (e.g., "too fatigued," or "very good overall") and any specific problems (e.g., "right knee pain toward the end of the run," or "back pain at the onset which disappeared mid-way through the workout")*

Some people like to add other items, such as weather conditions, distance, or pace. But don't be fooled into thinking that distance and pace, for example, are more important than the total time of your workout. They're not. Distance and pace relate to the quantity of the workout, but the time of exercise is related to its quality.

Exercise is also a form of meditation, and some people like to note the mental aspects of their workouts, which may be very separate from the physical aspects. For some people, working out is primarily a mental meditation session, and they wish to record the joyful, deep, and otherwise interesting thoughts and feelings they have during their workouts.

The most obvious type of equipment used in exercise includes stationary bikes, step machines, aerobic dance equipment, and the like. It is important to consider whether the equipment you use best matches your needs. If your exercise equipment matches your needs, you'll most likely enjoy the workout. I've seen many people persist in using exercise equipment that they truly dislike. Sometimes they don't like the equipment because it doesn't work properly. If it can't be fixed, or if you just don't like it, get rid of it. If you don't enjoying using it, find something else.

Any equipment can be useful as long as it matches your needs. If you're going to train aerobically, stationary and road bikes, treadmills, step machines, and other such gadgets can meet your needs. However, free weights or weight machines would be inappropriate.

Advertising convinces many people to use certain exercise equipment. Infomercials, TV and radio pitches, and print ads sell all kinds of machines. And a new one comes out almost every week. Most people who buy these devices either stop using them after the novelty wears off or never use them successfully.

The most inexpensive and perhaps most successful workout equipment is the equipment you naturally possess: your own body. Walking, jogging, running, swimming, and hiking are examples of natural activity. No machine will make your workout more effective than you can do with your own body.

Another important piece of equipment is footwear. This item, which may be one of the most important items for many people, is discussed in chapter 15.

Aerobic Base

If your program is not giving you the appropriate benefits, as described above and in part 1, you need to begin by building a good aerobic base. I would say that most people who exercise have never taken the time to build a good aerobic system. This is also the most

Frustration

Sally worked out five days a week, but every couple of months she would go a week or two in a row without doing any exercise at all. When asked why she was not consistent, Sally admitted that she was frustrated and depressed that her program was not working. She was still tired, she could not lose the excess body fat that had accumulated in recent years, and, although she was able to run faster now, she would often have nagging injuries, injuries she hadn't had before she began exercise.

Checking Sally's heart rate during her normal workout showed that her training was anaerobic. And she was allowing distance, not time, to determine the length of her workouts. At first it took her almost 45 minutes to run her three-mile course; now she was running the same course in just 30 minutes. So Sally's total workout time had diminished significantly. She also stated that her craving for sweets was greater, an indication that she was training her anaerobic (sugar-burning) system and not her aerobic (fat-burning) system.

Sally slowed her pace and increased her running time to 45 minutes. Within just two weeks she felt much better. Four months later, she had the confidence to attempt her goal of running a 10K (6.2-mile) race, which she completed with ease.

common problem I've seen in patients who have been exercising without success and with injury; they simply have not focused on developing their aerobic system. Persons who have a poor aerobic system may be under increased physical, chemical, or mental stress, or they may be exercising at too high a heart rate, or may have other problems described in chapter 4. Please review that chapter as necessary and make sure that all of your workouts are aerobic.

Developing your aerobic base will take three to four months, sometimes more. The most difficult obstacle during this period may be interference from other people, which may lead you to question yourself. "Is exercising this slow really going to help me?" is a common question. "Run with us just this one time" is also a common trap. As discussed earlier, it's vital that you be very strict in developing your aerobic base.

Direction and Measurement

You would never take a long trip without knowing how you were going to get there; often you have a map or other directions to follow. A "road map" is just as important for an exercise program. It's part of the fine tuning your body requires to obtain the benefits you desire. In addition to keeping track of your workouts by using a diary and building an aerobic base, the ability to plot out your direction by measuring your progress (discussed in chapter 7) is vital.

The MAF test provides the best and most practical measurement of your exercise progress. If you're not progressing, you're regressing. But if you don't know which direction you're moving in, it may be a long time before you find out that you've been slowly regressing. And then only after you've been injured, wasted months of exercise, or become overtrained.

If you're not getting results from exercise, something is not right. This may sound obvious, but millions of people continue exercising without realizing the benefits they expected. If this is the case with you, make the appropriate changes now.

13

Rehabilitation: Restoring Your Youth

> *Rehabilitation requires a very individual program. For this you need the help of a professional. It's still important to find the right starting point (type of activity) and intensity (heart rate).*

Research shows that exercise rehabilitation can greatly benefit individuals with heart disease, high blood pressure, or diabetes, not to mention individuals who are overweight. In addition, persons who have high blood cholesterol or osteoporosis, persons who are recovering from a broken bone, and persons suffering any number of other problems may greatly benefit from exercise.

Two important criteria must be met before exercise begins. First, you must be under the care of a doctor who can determine that your body is ready for the type of exercise you're about to undertake. Being under the care of the proper professional will mean that your rehabilitation will be individualized—tailored to your specific needs. You may need to work with a physical therapist or other professional in addition to your physician.

Second, you must find the proper starting point for your exercise. This might be the most basic level of exercise, such as walking in a swimming pool.

Quality of Life

We often hear about how much longer we're living, but what about the quality of those extra years? It's clear that exercise can improve and increase the quality of your life. For example, as we age, our nervous system loses some of its ability to function. This includes a loss of nerves and reduced capacity in those that are left. Our ligaments and tendons become less elastic, and muscle function is reduced, resulting in reduced reaction time and power. However, in those who are regularly active this decline is much less pronounced: a sixty-year-old person who is active may function like a forty-year-old. Studies have shown that older men who have been active for 20 years or more have reaction times equivalent to those of men who are in their twenties.

One large, long-term study showed that in addition to improving quality of life, aerobic exercise can actually add years to your life. The study also demonstrated that aerobic exercise countered such problems as cigarette smoking, obesity, and high blood pressure and reduced the overall death rate. People who exercised regularly realized more benefits. For example, the mortality rate among people who walked nine or more miles per week was 21 percent lower that that among people who walked three miles or less per week. What is more interesting, the mortality rate among those who worked out at a higher intensity (i.e., a higher heart rate) was higher than that among even their sedentary counterparts.

Other studies show that aerobic exercise can substantially reduce the risk of dying from cancer. The type of exercise that produced the most significant improvements was easy training, such as walking for 30 minutes several times a week.

Heart Disease

It's well known that smoking, high blood pressure, and high cholesterol can double your risk of heart disease. The fact is, persons who do not exercise regularly have the same or even a higher risk of developing heart disease. And for persons who have suffered a heart attack, exercise can substantially reduce the risk of death from a second heart attack.

Also, high-intensity exercise provides a small but very real risk of sudden death *during* exercise. Death during activity in individuals over the age of 30 usually results from atherosclerosis (the buildup of fat in the arteries), whereas in persons aged 30 or younger death during activity is more often due to a genetic enlargement of the heart or an aortic aneurysm.

Blood Fats

Most studies indicate that the reduced risk of heart disease resulting from exercise may be related to the reduced levels of blood cholesterol and triglycerides that result from exercise. Exercise may reduce the levels of total cholesterol and the so-called bad cholesterol (LDL) by only 10 percent. However, exercise may dramatically increase the level of the "good" cholesterol (HDL). It should be noted that not all studies show dramatic improvements in cholesterol levels from exercise; in these cases diet may be a factor. More importantly, most studies do show improvements in the ratios between LDL and HDL and between total cholesterol and HDL, reducing the risk of heart disease. Exercise also tends to reduce the level of triglycerides—another important fat in the blood.

Hypertension

Aerobic exercise can reduce blood pressure in persons with mild or moderate hypertension. It may be less effective in reducing blood pressure in persons with severe hypertension, perhaps due to a strong dietary connection. Properly monitoring your blood pressure is easy. It's also important to understand that blood pressure rises during exercise. The increase is not significant during easy aerobic exercise; however, during anaerobic training blood pressure may rise significantly. Your doctor may wish to check your blood pressure while you're walking on a treadmill or riding a stationary bike.

Blood-Sugar Problems

Aerobic exercise can greatly benefit persons suffering from diabetes and other blood-sugar problems. This may be because increased aerobic muscle development and reduced body fat—both of which result from aerobic exercise—help the body to utilize insulin and metabolize sugar more efficiently. It may also be because aerobic exercise reduces the body's resistance to insulin, one of the underlying problems in those with blood-sugar problems. However, individuals with blood-sugar problems must make improvements in their diet before the benefits from exercise will be significant. (The dietary aspect of treating blood-sugar problems is briefly discussed in chapter 20.)

Osteoporosis

A decrease in bone mass is another problem associated with aging. This is more often a problem in women, but men are not immune. For people over the age of 60 a loss of 30–50 percent of bone mass is possible. Weight-bearing exercises, such as walking, jogging, and running, can help in two ways. First, these exercises can slow the loss of bone. The sooner you begin exercising, the better your chances of preventing a loss of bone mass. More important for persons who already suffer from osteoporosis, weight-bearing exercise can increase bone mass, even in postmenopausal women. Exercises such as swimming, biking, and others that don't have a gravity-stress component are not as effective in helping prevent and correct osteoporosis.

Rehabilitation

Although patients with heart disease have unique problems, their rehabilitation is much like that of persons who have high blood pressure, high cholesterol and triglycerides, and other conditions discussed in this chapter. This section discusses the rehabilitation of persons with cardiac problems but can be useful for anyone requiring rehabilitation.

It is now clear that participation in a cardiac rehabilitation program substantially reduces the risk of death from another heart attack. This may be due to a variety of benefits. Exercise can improve circulation, not just in the skeletal and smooth muscles but in the heart itself. This increases the amount of blood going to the muscles, including the heart. Exercise also improves cardiac function, reducing stress on the heart. Other exercise benefits are associated with improvements in the levels of blood pressure, blood glucose, blood fats, and stress.

Perhaps the second most important recommendation for persons involved in a rehabilitation program, after being cleared by their doctor, is that they wear a heart rate monitor. This will prevent them from exercising at too high a heart rate, putting excess stress on the heart and the rest of the body, which further increases stress from anaerobic exercise. This is most likely to occur in the first stages of rehabilitation. Studies have shown that as their exercise program progresses and they begin to see benefits, cardiac patients may not be active enough, perhaps because they are too conservative, and their heart rate stays too low. This results in a plateau in benefits. In this stage of rehabilitation the heart rate monitor assures that the patient exercises with enough intensity. In calculating your optimal aerobic heart rate using the 180-Formula, after subtracting your age from 180 be sure to subtract another 10 beats, as specified for persons recovering from a major illness.

Walking may be the best starting point for anyone involved in rehabilitation. If you choose walking as your starting point, it's best to follow the guidelines discussed in chapter 11—rehabilitation is truly a new beginning. For some patients even easy walking may be too stressful, in which case walking in a pool can be helpful.

Walking in Water

Another great exercise for those in rehabilitation is walking in a swimming pool. Ideally, the water should come up to the person's waist or chest. This allows some gravity stress, although half or more of the person's weight bearing will be reduced because of buoyancy. In this case, walking back and forth in the pool or performing other easy movements is acceptable.

One problem for persons wishing to perform water workouts is finding a pool that is accessible. If you have a local pool, it may be reserved for swimming laps only. However, "water aerobics" and other types of water activities are becoming more popular. Waterproof heart rate monitors are available for such activities. Be sure to ask about easy access into and out of the pool, which may be a concern for people with certain disabilities.

Some individuals may have special needs beyond those described above:

- *For patients who are recovering from a broken bone or have osteoporosis, performing weight-bearing exercises is a must. The only exception is persons with very recent fractures; once their doctor has given them permission to exercise, they should proceed cautiously, for obvious reasons. However, in these cases, more stress can usually be tolerated by a previously injured bone than most people are willing to place on it. Individuals with very recent fractures may find that walking is the best exercise to start with. However, if it's too early in the healing process to walk, they should begin by walking in a pool and gradually progress to normal walking.*

- *Individuals recovering from replacement of a hip, knee, or other joint should begin by walking in a swimming pool and gradually progress to walking on dry land.*

- *Persons with hypertension, high blood triglycerides, or blood-sugar problems may have too many carbohydrates in their diet. They must reduce their carbohydrate intake in combination with proper exercise for optimal results (see chapter 20).*

14

Changing with
the Seasons

*Many individuals may find that chang-
ing their workout with each season
helps keep the excitement in their program and avoid periods of inactivity.
This chapter discusses approaches for
each of the four seasons. It also discusses the common problem of seasonal affective disorder (SAD), which is
related to the winter blues—how to
recognize it, how to prevent it, and how
to treat it with exercise.*

For some people, following the same routine year-round can get
monotonous. Others identify a workout that suits them, whether
it is walking, jogging, or cycling, and are happy to stick with that
activity, no matter what time of year and despite adverse weather.
Triathletes, for example (who swim, bike, and run) enjoy the three
different activities they regularly perform. Runners (who often perform little or no other exercise) are just as content in a single sport.
For those who need a change, seasonal variation of activity can be
the answer.

Spring

Many people look forward to spring, when they can get outdoors again after what always seems like a long winter. The number of hours of daylight and the temperature increase. The conditions are perfect for exercising outdoors.

Walking, jogging, and running always seem more enjoyable in the spring. The increased daylight makes it easier to work out in the morning, before your day begins, or after work without having to worry about darkness and the dangers that may accompany it. Outdoor biking, however, may still be challenging because although the temperatures are great for walking or running, they are still low enough to make the wind chill a factor. A temperature of 48°F may be fine for walking, but a wind chill of 36°F may make biking uncomfortable for some.

For those who have been working out in a gym, at home, or in some other indoor location getting outside can be a refreshing change. But if you're also going to change your specific activity, be careful. Any change in activity should be made slowly, easily, and with caution. Even though you've built up your aerobic system on a stationary bike, you may encounter problems if you start jogging. The muscles used in these two activities are different enough that a sudden switch to jogging might place a significant stress on those muscles, ligaments, and joints, with the real potential for overuse injury.

One problem with making this type of transition is that you may be aerobically fit and not realize that changing from the bike to jogging involves the stress that it does. Your heart rate does not rise much, you don't breathe hard, and you feel that you can jog with ease. But it will take a few short weeks to really adapt. Switching from a bike to a walk is much easier and less risky. Here are some healthful ways to accomplish more significant changes:

- *If your transition is from a stationary bike to jogging or running, be sure to perform a good warm-up by walking. Start with a slow walk, gradually increasing the pace, and after your warm-up period begin jogging (and if you are in good enough shape, progress to running). The cooldown should be just the opposite: jog slower at the onset, but spend more time walking to the end of the workout.*

- *If you're riding your bike outside, and you've been indoors on a stationary bike, you should have little or no trouble. Indoor bikes come in two basic varieties: the more traditional stationary bike and your own outdoor bike placed on a trainer (or rollers). The latter is best since that's what your body is used to riding. If you're changing from a stationary bike to a different outdoor bike, allow about two weeks for the slight adaptation your body must make, training for a little less time at a reduced intensity.*

- *If you've been swimming all winter and decide to start a spring program of walking, jogging, or running, any of which would represent a more extreme mechanical change for your body, you'll need more time to adapt to your spring exercise. You should allow three to four weeks. During this period of adaptation you should train more slowly and for a slightly shorter period of time.*

Whatever the change, consider that if the new activity involves different mechanics, your body will need a short period to adjust. The more significant the change, the longer it will take.

Another consideration regarding springtime exercise is that people are naturally more active in the spring. The phrase "spring cleaning" says it all. If you do more physical work outside—cleaning your yard, basement, or garage or performing other springtime chores, you may have to reduce the time of each workout or take some days off from exercise. Otherwise you just add more activity to your exercise schedule, which could lead to overtraining. In general, for every hour you spend on spring cleaning, reduce your exercise time by about 20–30 minutes. This will prevent you from overtraining and ensure that you maintain your aerobic system.

For competitive athletes spring is often a time of racing, tournaments, and matches. These activities place additional stress on your body—stress you should be able to handle. Properly building and maintaining yourself during the winter should lead to no adverse results. However, adding competitive events to your existing schedule, along with other outdoor work, may make it impossible for you to maintain the right balance. Even if you're only adding competitions to your spring schedule, you should reduce your total training time. A general rule is to add one rest day (no exercise) for each day of competition. It's best to schedule this rest day for the day before competition, making sure you warm up well on the day of competition.

Summer

In many areas of the United States summer brings high heat and humidity. The phrase "hazy, hot, and humid" becomes a commonplace on the news. High heat and humidity place significant stress on your body. I've seen many people try to maintain their outdoor schedule, especially during July and August, only to become increasingly exhausted.

If the weather is hot and humid, try to exercise in the early morning or evening, or work out indoors if possible. In addition, consider reducing your total workout time by about 25 percent. These changes will help assure that you don't become overtrained due to the addition of significant weather stress. Working out indoors will allow you to avoid the weather stress—and the bugs. Summer is like winter in that both are times when avoiding the weather by training indoors has some benefits.

If you're a competitive athlete, you should make these changes in addition to the changes recommended for springtime competition. Thus, if you are competing during the hot summer months, your total training time may be very low. You'll have no trouble maintaining your winter and spring training benefits throughout the summer if you've built a good aerobic base. And you'll compete better, and won't suffer any setbacks in the fall.

Fall

The fall is usually a time of great weather. We also tend to associate September with the start of a new school year, but in a sense it's almost like January 1—the beginning of a new year. Compared with the hecticness of summer, fall seems like a time of stability. As a result, fall is a time when many people begin exercise for the first time or make adjustments to their existing program. Like springtime, fall is a time when most people want to be outdoors as much as possible, if only to get outdoor chores done before the onset of winter.

With the fall season comes diminishing daylight. You may need to more carefully plan your morning or evening outdoor workouts: you don't want to get caught in the dark while riding, walking, or running unless you're in a safe location.

The end of the fall can be a time of vulnerability. That vulnerability has to do with the oncoming physical, chemical, and mental stress of the holidays, as well as the physical stress of colder weather. You should aim to develop a solid training routine, with as few distractions as possible, by November so that you will be able to maintain your program despite the stresses of cold weather and especially the holiday period, which won't end until the first of January.

Winter

The potential holiday stress continues into the winter. It's compounded by reduced daylight and colder temperatures. It's the time when more people let their regular exercise slide and quickly get out of shape, when in fact it is a time when exercise is especially important as a way to combat stress.

For many people cold weather in itself is enough of a stress, leading those who dislike the cold to exercise less in winter. Working out indoors can solve this problem, especially if you work out at home or if you don't have to drive in bad weather to go to the gym. This is a time when home exercise works best for many people. If you walk or jog, consider going to a mall or a large shopping center. Some malls now open their doors for walkers before regular business hours (it's actually a way of attracting more potential customers; just don't window shop while working out).

One of the most commonly heard complaints about winter is that it's the time when people gain weight. That's due in part to poor eating habits (much more sugar than usual) but in part to diminished activity and increased stress. Not counting exercise, most people are less active in the winter. Combine that with less exercise, or even the abandonment of your program, and it's easy to see how the weight, in the form of body fat, is gained. When January comes, many people have "lose weight" and "exercise" at the top of their list of New Year's resolutions.

Another way of looking at the seasons is to consider spring and fall, and summer and winter, as two separate periods instead of four. In many parts of the country the summer and winter weather can sometimes be harsh, hot and humid in the summer and cold in the winter. This is a time to work out indoors. In the spring and fall outdoor exercise is predominant.

Dressing for Successful Exercise

An important consideration is how to dress for exercise. I'm not referring to the latest trend, or wearing colors that "match." Rather than spending money on expensive exercise clothes, buy a heart monitor, a treadmill, or other practical items.

The most important concern regarding dress for exercise is not fashion but physiology. Improper dressing can adversely affect how your body burns fat. Specifically, if you heat your body too much, you'll reduce your ability to burn body fat. This has to do with the body's stores of brown fat.

Our bodies possess two distinct types of body fat: brown and white. Both fat stores are active, living parts of our body, heavily influenced by diet and exercise. Most of our fat stores consist of white fat, typically making up from 10 percent to as much as 50 percent of our weight. This fat serves mainly as an energy reserve.

Brown fat stores make up only about 1 percent of our body weight. Depending on how it is stimulated, brown fat may help regulate our fat burning. It can make you gain weight and become sluggish in the winter, like a hibernating animal, or if your caloric intake is too low, brown fat can slow the burning of white fat.

Brown fat is largely controlled by temperature. The cooler the skin around brown fat stores, the more those stores are activated and the more white fat you burn. If you get too hot during the day or when you exercise because of overdressing (or a warm environment), your brown-fat activity may decrease, resulting in less white fat burned.

For these reasons, you should avoid wearing too many clothes during exercise. That you'll lose more weight if you sweat more is a common weight-loss myth. True, the scale will show that you've lost weight because you've lost water, often to the point of dehydration. But overdressing in order to sweat more can actually reduce fat burning.

Another important feature of brown fat is that it's stimulated by cold. Cooling your brown-fat areas can help stimulate the burning of white fat. Brown fat is found around the shoulders and under the arms, between the ribs and at the nape of the neck. Don't get chilled when working out, but wear little enough to allow the cool air to stimulate your skin. Also, end your after-workout shower with up to a minute of cool to cold water.

Going to a hot tub, sauna, or steam room after exercise can offset some of the fat-burning benefits of exercise in the same way as overdressing during exercise. If you want to use the hot tub or other heating routines, take a cool to cold shower or cold tub bath afterward.

Thus, if you exercise in a cool environment, wear two layers so that you can remove one layer when your body gets warmed up. Typically, people dress for their immediate comfort. For example, people going outdoors for a walk in cold weather "dress warm." While that is a wise thing to do, once you warm up, you should remove some clothing so that you won't become too warm; however, don't allow yourself to get chilled.

SAD

What used to be called "cabin fever" in some parts of the country and "winter blues" in other parts is now referred to as seasonal affective disorder, or SAD. This widely recognized condition is associated with adrenal stress. It's a functional disorder that affects some people during the winter months due to the reduced sunlight and perhaps the cold weather as well.

Symptoms associated with SAD occur in the fall and winter months. The most common ones include the following:

- *depression*

- *poor sleep patterns*

- *lowered energy*

- *reduced libido*

- *decreased physical capacity*

- *increased cravings for carbohydrates*

- *impaired social functioning*

In a study of sixty-five college athletes, almost half were classified as having some form of SAD. Some only had more minor symptoms, a condition referred to as "subsyndromal seasonal affective disorder."

Light therapy has been used successfully to treat or prevent this problem. If you suffer from this problem, it is important to spend some time outdoors in the fall and winter. If you've joined a gym to avoid the cold weather, take a short walk at midday, if possible, to get some exposure to daylight. Although stimulation through the eyes is important, getting light on your skin can also be effective, according to new research. Whatever the case, if you're bundled up and wearing sunglasses, or any type of glasses or contact lenses for that matter, you won't take in much light.

In addition to natural light from the sun, consider using "full spectrum" light bulbs in as many indoor work and living areas as possible. These light bulbs are now readily available in many different types and sizes.

While some people can perform the same exercise year-round, many must change with the seasons. If they don't, their exercise consistency is reduced, sometimes to the point of inactivity. This typically occurs during the winter months, sometimes due to holiday and weather stress. SAD also impacts these problems. Exercise outdoors in the winter can solve both problems.

15

Exercise Footwear: Finding the Right Shoe

Do you find it difficult to believe that popular exercise shoes actually can be harmful? The information about this topic as described here is from research studies rather than from magazines. Most people hear only about the so-called benefits of shoes through magazines and ads. Unfortunately, magazine articles are often shaped by the shoe companies that buy advertising space. For fear of losing advertising dollars, magazines rarely—if ever—report on studies that show exercise shoes to be harmful.

Scientific studies (see the bibliography) have clearly shown that most modern exercise shoes, especially the expensive ones or the overprotective types, can cause injuries. Although going barefoot is best, if you really want to wear shoes when you exercise, finding the *right* shoes for protection is not a complex task. However, the first step is listening to your instincts and science rather than all the marketing hype. Once you find the type of shoe that is best for you, the next step is to find a shoe that fits you properly. The majority of exercisers wear improperly fitting shoes, which also contributes to injury.

Most people who exercise wear exercise shoes when working out, and many people who don't work out also wear exercise shoes. Exercise shoes help to protect the foot from the potentially damaging effects of stones, glass, and other objects, and sometimes they even protect the top of the foot from injury if it is stepped on during a basketball or other game. Most people believe that these often expensive shoes also provide the extra support and stability necessary to prevent injury. Unfortunately, the opposite may be the case, *since modern exercise footwear has been associated with frequent injury.* In fact, barefoot athletes generally receive fewer injuries than do athletes wearing shoes. Even worse is that some people erroneously believe that advanced athletic footwear can improve athletic function.

Ankle sprains may be the most common sports injuries and may account for a greater loss of playing time than any other injury. Foot and ankle imbalances, many of which are asymptomatic, can cause a variety of secondary problems in the leg, knee, hip, pelvis, spine, and even areas higher in the body. These foot and ankle imbalances may also result from wearing modern footwear.

There are hundreds of exercise shoes on the market. Most people think that the best, most protective shoes are the more expensive ones. Contrary to this belief, however, studies show that *the more expensive running shoes are actually associated with more than twice as many injuries as the cheapest shoes.*

The modern athletic shoe, with medial-arch support and a relatively thick, soft sole, can be a hazard in part due to the shock-absorbing and impact-cushioning materials used in it. Popular athletic shoes are not engineered to fit the human foot, and studies have shown that, for every injury caused by plain, inexpensive shoes, there are 123 caused by more expensive, athletic shoes. Materials that increase the height of the shoe's sole and rigid or semi-rigid construction that interferes with normal foot and ankle movement also increase your risk of injury.

How Shoes Can Cause Stress

When you're exercising on your feet, or even just walking or working during the day, the weight bearing of the lower extremity normally produces a sharp rise in impact, or vertically transmitted force from the foot and ankle up the leg. This normal stress induced by the impact of your foot is the common denominator in injuries to the foot, ankle, leg, and knee. For example, the normal force on impact during running is about 2.5 times your body weight. If you don't adapt to this impact, injuries such as plantar fasciitis, shin splints, stress fractures, metatarsalgia, and even osteoarthritis (including knees, hips, and spine), and various knee problems can occur. Even workouts such as cycling produce the same impact forces, but the *rate* of loading is lower. Researchers S. Robbins and A. M. Hanna state in their 1987 article on injuries related to running that the "high injury frequency in sports involving running and jumping has led many to conclude that the lower extremities, particularly the foot to be of poor design, an unusually fragile structure unable to sustain the use associated with running without injury, thus requiring additional protective devices." Thus the boom in the manufacture and marketing of the so-called highly technological and very expensive athletic shoe. This implied inability of the human frame to function effectively during natural activity is illogical, as Robbins and Hanna say: "The opinion that the lower extremities are inherently fragile goes against the authors' understanding of the concept of natural selection."

Thick-soled, soft shoes force the foot into a more rigid position and keep it from adapting naturally to the stress induced by sports activity. This adversely affects muscle function, as first shown as long ago as 1954 by researchers Basmajian and Bentzon, whose electromyographic (EMG) studies demonstrated, by measuring the electrical activity of the muscles, a lack of normal muscle function in persons wearing exercise shoes. Perhaps this is why North American runners experience a higher rate of injury than runners from Europe, Asia, the West Indies, and Haiti, where barefoot athletes are more common. Heel counters can also be a problem, causing reduced functioning of the gastrocnemius, soleus, and quadriceps muscles during the heel strike.

Thus, a primary reason for higher injury rates in those wearing exercise shoes is the reduced sensory feedback to the brain from the foot, *while the same level of shock absorption is present.* The brain must always know where the rest of the body is during exercise (or any activity) in order to properly compensate. This position awareness, or proprioception, is derived almost entirely from muscle and tactile receptors in the feet. This may be another mechanism by which *muscular inhibition* in the foot and leg can significantly contribute to structural imbalance and secondary injury. This position awareness normally declines with age as a result of a loss of plantar tactile sensitivity and may be a contributing factor in the increased frequency of falls in later life. *But today even young athletes wearing modern footwear show no kinesthetic awareness.* This could result in a significantly greater number of hip fractures in coming generations.

That exercise shoes do not significantly reduce the effects of shock absorption during activity is a significant aspect of increased injury in those who wear them. Activity performed while barefoot normally produces significant communication with the brain (via the nervous system) from the bottom of the foot. We rely on this information so that we will adjust our posture and gait to provide compensation for the stress of the activity. Wearing a shoe prevents the transmission of this sensation. The load created by a barefoot athlete allows the foot to absorb shock naturally, and without injury, a process that is inhibited by shoes.

Arch Function

Members of populations that tend to live barefoot have a natural high arch that significantly flattens during weight-bearing activities. Many people confuse this normal response by the body with "flat feet" or improperly refer to it as a "pronation problem." The arch response in those who wear overprotective shoes is not the same, possibly because the arch support common to most athletic shoes blocks the normal sensation in the feet. When this sensation is inhibited, a higher amount of stress is placed on the foot, ankle, and other parts of the body.

Taping and Other Joint Support

Ankle taping may help prevent injuries, but not through immobilization, as was once thought. Taping may prevent injuries by tractioning the skin of the foot and leg, compensating for the lost sensation in the foot that occurs when overprotective shoes are worn. *If taping is used as a therapy, it may be necessary to include the lower leg, ankle, and plantar areas.* And rather than the many layers of tape that are commonly applied, as few as two or three strips of tape wrapped around the ankle and foot, anchored on the lower leg, may be effective. Nor is it necessary to tape the foot tightly.

Taping the ankles may help prevent injury by *partially restoring* the impaired proprioception caused by modern athletic footwear. This may be the primary benefit provided by taping since *the support function is lost after as little as 20 minutes.* Studies show that proprioception is 107.5 percent worse in nontaped subjects wearing athletic footwear, and 58.1 percent worse in taped subjects wearing athletic footwear, than in subjects who are barefoot.

In general, the use of tape and other support devices reduces your joints' range of motion and can impair athletic performance. This can take the form of reduced speed, agility, and vertical jumping and reduced force production and total work output—something to consider if you're going to compete. In addition, the use of prophylactic devices for other joints may *increase* the incidence of injury. For example, numerous studies clearly demonstrate that knee supports of various types increase the incidence of knee injury.

Orthotics (braces or supports for weak joints or muscles) are usually plastic or leather shoe inserts that are specially made. Although they've become popular in recent years, studies have not shown them to be effective, since most of the benefits of foot orthotics are empirical. This does not necessarily discount their effectiveness. One potential problem with the use of orthotic devices is that the need for other therapies may be overlooked. For those individuals with past or current surgical needs, stroke or hemiparetic patients, or those who will, for various reasons, never have normal foot function, orthotic devices may be very important in the rehabilitation process.

Neither general shoe inserts nor orthotics, including those with shock-absorbing abilities, have been shown to protect against the risks of injury. *These devices may actually further reduce arch function and provide excessive cushioning, resulting in increased structural stress.* Studies fail to show that orthotics have any significant impact on the muscles in the leg and foot. These and other factors have led most researchers to believe that these devices also do not prevent injuries.

Other Ankle Dysfunction

Ankle problems are among the most common athletic injuries. One study showed that during a two-year period 78 percent of basketball players experienced some type of ankle injury. Of these, 83 percent reported *recurrent* ankle problems. Many basketball players and other people wear "high-top" athletic shoes, thinking that they provide additional ankle support. However, clinical trials have not demonstrated that this is the case. Studies show that *high-top athletic shoes were associated with increased rates of injury.* One study showed that high-top shoes could increase the risk of ankle sprains. Participants wearing high-top shoes found that they had *a lower average jump height and needed more time to complete a running course* in comparison with participants who wore low-support shoes.

Consider the following:

- *In many cases, the use of inexpensive, flat, nonsupportive athletic shoes may be best for exercise, even during competition, and whenever shoes are worn. These are made by lesser-known companies and cost up to ten times less than the more popular, more sought-after brands.*

- *Most major shoe companies make some flat, less supportive, and less cushioned shoes that may be an improvement over their oversupported and cushioned ones.*

- *You may benefit from spending more time shoeless. This does not necessarily mean during exercise, unless you're used to exercising barefoot, but during idle time or when it is appropriate to remove your shoes (i.e., at home or in some working conditions).*

- *Being barefoot will help the muscles, ligaments, and tendons adapt to a new, more natural position of the foot, especially important for those athletes who have spent almost their entire lifetime in shoes with a higher heel. This is the same process women who have worn high-heeled dress shoes throughout their career encounter when they decide (often in response to lower-back or other problems) to switch to flatter shoes. This process can be started with the removal of the insert found in most shoes, which can reduce some cushioning and height and improve the fit of the shoe (see below).*

- *Athletes sponsored by shoe companies should consider switching to more appropriate footwear, but if none is available, they should ask the shoe company to make them a special shoe appropriate for their foot and sport.*

- *Peer pressure may be a significant factor in athletes' choice of shoes. This is especially true in kids. For example, a high-school basketball player may be reluctant to wear low-top shoes when everyone else wears high-tops.*

Proper Shoe Fit

Shoes that do not fit properly are another potential source of significant structural stress. Subtle imbalances resulting from improper athletic shoe fit can cause significant and more obvious

How to Buy Athletic Shoes

- *Always measure both feet while standing on a hard floor. Most adults don't measure their feet when buying new shoes, even though their size may have changed. Consequently, they often wear the wrong size for years, even decades. You may have to measure your shoe size two or three times during a day to note size fluctuations. (Any significant fluctuations must be differentiated from serious health problems, such as significant swelling or pathological changes.) The largest measurement should be used as a general guide when buying shoes. However, there are no standard sizes; manufacturers vary their sizes.*

- *Allow time for a proper fitting. Find a hard surface to walk on (carpet can make shoes feel more comfortable), going outside if necessary. Try on a shoe in the size you normally wear. Even if it feels good, try the next half-size larger. Continue to increase the size by a half-size until you find a pair that obviously is too large and then go back to the previous half-size. That's usually the best fit. Remember to try on shoes with varying widths as necessary.*

- *It may be best to wear shoes in two different sizes if the variance between your feet is more than a half-size. If the variance is less than one half-size, fit the larger foot.*

- *Many women find that men's exercise shoes fit better than women's. However, the shoe must fit properly. Some women's feet do not fit men's shoes, and some stores do not carry men's shoes in sizes small enough to fit women.*

- *Be prepared to shop at more than one store. Most outlets carry only some of the many shoes on the market. Mail-order shoe outlets may be less expensive, but often you need to return shoes until you find the correct size.*

- *When you find a shoe that fits properly, buy several pairs. Shoes are manufactured based on style, color, and other marketing trends, so any one shoe may not be around for long. When buying multiple pairs of a shoe, try on each pair, as size may vary slightly.*

problems higher in the body structure—in the knees, hips, lower back, or even higher. In a survey of more than 100 runners I discovered that 52 percent exercised in shoes that were too small. To discover whether you are wearing improperly fitting shoes, pull out the manufacturer's insert and look for abnormal wear patterns. You should be able to see the full imprint of all five toes; if you can see the imprint of only three-quarters of the big toe, for example, it may be jamming into the front of the shoe rather than comfortably resting on the floor of the shoe. If this is the case, you may also have an irritated metatarsal joint (just behind the big toe), which may be very sensitive to touch. If you show signs of the infamous "black toenail syndrome" found in many runners, look for wear and tear in the front of the shoe: the nail of the big toe may be trying to push through the end of the shoe, indicating that the shoe is too short.

Taking the time not only to educate yourself about exercise shoes, including avoiding the hype by shoe companies, but also to get the right fit can make exercise a more effective and enjoyable process. It can also help you avoid the injuries associated with improper footwear.

16

Anatomy of an Injury

*The right exercise program has thera-
peutic benefits; it can correct certain
injuries as well as prevent future ones. It is
also important to understanding what
causes injuries, including muscle imbalance, joint dysfunction, and asymptomatic injuries. This chapter explains the
injury process and discusses which types
of professionals are best suited to treat
specific conditions. It also suggests a
variety of easy, safe, and effective remedies for nagging problems that you can
treat without the help of a professional.*

Every exerciser's worst nightmare is an injury. Unfortunately, it
is a common occurrence especially among persons performing
anaerobic exercise and among persons who do not warm up properly. Even more unfortunate is that most people believe that being
injured is part of the workout game. This is not the case. If you
exercise properly, you should never experience injuries (with the
rare exception of trauma).

If you do get injured, it means that you've done something
wrong; the injury may be the result of training, diet, nutrition,

NSAIDs

Many people take aspirin and other nonsteroidal anti-inflammatory drugs (NSAIDs) when they are injured. Although NSAIDs may provide some benefits in some cases, they can also interfere with the normal healing process. NSAIDs can reduce inflammation, which conversely is an important part of recovery and healing. By inhibiting the migration of white blood cells to sites of injury and by disrupting other actions that can reduce inflammation, NSAIDs impair the healing process. This may delay tissue healing and impair scar formation, thereby resulting in diminished strength of the mature scar. In addition, NSAIDs can cause other problems when it comes to healing:

- *NSAIDs may inhibit the repair process of fracture healing, since the first critical stage of this process involves inflammation.*
- *NSAIDs are commonly associated with an increased incidence of gastric and duodenal ulcers, gastrointestinal bleeding, and increased morbidity and mortality.*
- *The prevalence of intestinal ulcers in people using NSAIDs for at least six months may be as high as 44 percent.*
- *Intestinal blood flow may be reduced in those taking NSAIDs, which could adversely affect digestion and especially absorption of nutrients.*
- *The use of NSAIDs can produce muscle dysfunction and exaggerated exercise-associated muscle damage.*
- *The consensus of studies does not show that NSAIDs adequately reduce delayed-onset muscle soreness (DOMS).*
- *NSAIDs can adversely affect cartilage repair, especially osteoarthritic cartilage.*
- *NSAIDs may cause kidney damage, especially in those who are dehydrated.*
- *NSAIDs, especially aspirin, acetaminophen, and ibuprofen, can interfere with normal sleep patterns, including suppression of melatonin and changes in body temperature.*
- *Reye's syndrome (potentially fatal in children, causing liver, neurological, and mitochondrial damage) has been associated with aspirin and other salicylate use when taken during viral infection.*
- *Other side effects of NSAID use can include headaches, skin rash, tinnitus, and drowsiness.*

stress, or some other factor. Let's look at a typical injury and determine where it originated and how it developed. But first you should be familiar with the three basic, usually overlapping types of injuries—structural (also called physical or mechanical), chemical, and mental.

The Structural Injury

You awaken for your morning workout, and as you bend to get into your shoes you feel a little twinge in your right hamstrings. Nothing more than that. But several days later, there it is again, now a bit more noticeable. And that evening the twinge turned annoyance begins to be painful. The next day's workout is hindered, and by the following week you are feeling real pain. Now your hip doesn't seem to move right, and your knee is throbbing. After another week all the pain has settled around the knee. You recall no trauma, your shoes are good, and you've not changed training routines.

This "domino effect" takes place in millions of exercisers throughout the world. An injury originating in some seemingly benign event evolves into a real impairment. But there's logic to your body; changes don't occur for no reason at all. With some exceptions, an injury is simply the end result of a series of dominos falling over; one little, innocuous problem leading to another, and so on. The end result, sometimes after a half-dozen or so dominos have fallen, is a symptom. Depending on how the body adapts and compensates to the falling dominos, that symptom may be pain, dysfunction, loss of power.

Let's go back to the example of the person who develops knee pain. This is a very common injury. From a professional standpoint, there are two ways to approach a knee problem.

The traditional view, and in recent decades the more popular approach, attempts to name the condition. For example, if the pain is more lateral and especially if it is located a bit above the knee joint, it may be labeled "ilio-tibial band syndrome" (ITB). Even worse, if the patient is a runner, the problem is called "runner's knee." This senseless attempt to name the symptoms does not address how the problem occurred, how to recover from the problem, or how to prevent it from recurring once it is corrected. (Of course, some injuries—a broken bone or a ruptured spinal disc, for example—are more clearly defined and require medical intervention.)

This approach also assumes that each "bursitis," say, is exactly the same as every other one. And modern medicine has an off-the-shelf treatment for each named problem—from rest to stretching, heat to cold, anti-inflammatory drugs to surgery. The most indefensible aspect of this cookbook approach is that many professionals know what they're going to do to you before they even see you. Look up the name of your problem in the medical books, and you'll find your remedy. It's a classic case of treating the symptom and ignoring the cause—and the person attached.

The alternative approach is to look at the whole person and, much like Sherlock Holmes, discover the circumstances that led to the big event, the symptom. These provide vital clues to how the problem developed, and therefore how to avoid it in the future, and how to correct the real cause of the injury. This approach views each injury as part of the athlete and each person as a unique individual with specific needs. Anything less is an insult to the human body.

So just how does the symptom of knee pain evolve? Of course, our example is just one person's paradigm. The same knee pain could develop in a dozen different ways for as many individuals. But lets replace this over-simplified description with a real-life scenario.

Our athlete awakens one morning, puts on his shoes for a workout, and feels the first symptom: a twinge in the hamstring muscles of his right leg. But this is not the beginning of the problem. The first domino could have fallen, long before this first manifestation, possibly months earlier. Perhaps the left foot underwent microtrauma as the result of a training shoe that felt fine but did not fit properly. This common problem results in a structural stress in the foot and ankle. While this produced no symptoms, it did affect, in a very adverse way, the mechanics of the left ankle. As often happens when there is this type of mechanical stress on the body, the brain senses the problem and attempts to adapt. In this case, perhaps compensation took place through the bones and muscles in the pelvis. Specifically, the pelvis tilted to modify its movement so that weight bearing decreased on the side of the body where the stress was felt and increased on the opposite side, where the symptom will eventually show up. But not yet.

The increased weight bearing on the right side may cause some of the muscles in the thigh to become overworked. This may also occur due to the gait change resulting from the tilt in the pelvis. The result is a "short leg," another commonly named symptom, on the right side. The quadriceps, through an unsuccessful attempt to compensate for the mechanical stress in the pelvis, may become weaker or inhibited. And finally, the opposite muscles—the hamstrings—compensate for the quad problem by tightening.

Bending forward to put on your right shoe requires the hamstrings to gently stretch. But when they are too tight and you ask them to do their job anyway, they can become overstretched and develop micro-tears. This is the form of that slight twinge.

So what could we propose as therapy for our patient's knee pain? Anti-inflammatory drugs? Ice on the knee? The answer is obvious now that the whole picture is apparent. We must correct the original problem. In this case, the first domino to fall was a shoe that was not right for the foot that went into it. Whether all the dominos will line up on their own if you pick up the first one depends on the person and how much damage was done. Generally, the body has a great natural ability to heal itself, even to correct the lingering inflammation in the knee. And in many cases this is just what takes place when the cause of the problem is corrected.

How can you avert problems before they begin? Questioned about an injury, many people suggest clues, for example, that their shoes may not fit. It may be a passing thought, a subconscious note, but it's there. And most people can suggest possible causes for their injuries; however, most ignore or don't recognize the clues. Learning how to read your body comes in time and is worth the effort.

More importantly, when your body gives you a very obvious sign, such as a hamstring twinge, it's time to STOP. Assess what's going on, or it may quickly become too late. Waiting until you're physically unable to work out—the point where your body forces you to stop—only results in time wasted and unnecessary damage.

And finally, this whole process, from the time the first domino falls, may take weeks or months, and in some cases years. And throughout this entire process your performance is adversely affected.

The Chemical Injury

You try to fit your workouts into your day juggling work, family, and social life. But now it's getting harder to get through the day because of fatigue. And training no longer energizes you. You're more irritable than ever. The few pounds you've gained, the first in some time, are probably due to the ravenous appetite you've recently acquired. And you're on your third cold in six months. If you could only sleep as well as you used to. "Luckily I'm not injured," you tell your exercise partners.

Well, my friend, you are injured. But the injury is different from the structural impairments we're familiar with, such as knee pain. This is a chemical injury. Chemical injuries typically don't produce the kinds of pains their mechanical counterparts produce. However, some may provide symptoms of inflammation, which can be painful. By far the most common characteristic of a chemical problem is fatigue. Either the cause of the fatigue or the fatigue itself may in turn produce other chemical symptoms like the ones just described.

Let's look at the options open to you when you have these symptoms. The evidence includes fatigue, irritability, increased weight gain and hunger, colds, and insomnia.

As in the case of any injury, the first step is to rule out more serious conditions, such as anemia, infections, or other more serious disorders. This is often easily accomplished with the right blood tests, a proper history, and a physical exam. And when the lab report is found normal, we've taken the first step in the right direction. Genuine diseases most likely don't exist.

Once diseases are ruled out, more conservative methods can be considered. But wait: we must consider whether the symptoms are all in our patient's head. Is it a psychological memory she's having, related to a past experience? An unpleasant episode with training wheels as a girl? Let's conclude that this is not the case.

In a patient who has a whole inventory of symptoms that are adversely affecting lifestyle, there is usually a common chemical scenario of cause and effect. So it is with someone we'll call "Anne."

Perhaps the problem originated when her schedule—not just

the training log but all of the hours of the day—got too full. The word many people use when they try to describe how full their schedule is provides a vital clue to what is going on: *juggling*. Anne is squeezing things into her schedule all the items of the day, including exercise. For many, this offends the body's ability to recover properly. And as the months go by, a recuperative deficit, or stress, builds up.

Let's try to reconstruct the events that may have led to this chemical injury. Perhaps a desire to lose weight led our patient to increase her training. Undoubtedly, she increased not only her total workout time but also the intensity of her workouts. Add to that the stress of rushing meals, and dashing from home to work, from workout to home, and so on, and you get the picture.

Initially, Anne's adrenal glands probably tolerated the increased stress reasonably well. After all, that's their job. But like a long event you're not trained for, the vicious cycle of work, family, social life, and exercise probably became too much to keep up with. Soon, there must have been less time to do the things that needed to be done, and thus recovery was hindered. As Anne attempted to keep up with her schedule, eventually her adrenal glands must have reached the point when they could not effectively deal with all the stress. At this point, proper recovery likely came to a halt.

When the adrenals are not able to keep up, the bodily functions they maintain begin to decline. The blood sugar becomes unstable, which may produce symptoms of fatigue. Also, when the brain is deprived of the sugar it needs, cravings and increased hunger follow. And not only the brain but the whole nervous system is sensitive to relatively small changes in blood sugar, which often leads to irritability.

Because of the influence the adrenal glands have on other hormonal systems of the body, when the adrenals become less effective the metabolism may slow down. And this may be accompanied by a shift in fuel usage—more sugar and less fat—which can result in more stored fat and decreased endurance. Inevitably, hunger intensifies, fatigue worsens, and the cycle continues.

Excess adrenal stress is frequently accompanied by decreased immunity. When the body's defense system is suppressed, colds, flu, and even allergies become more common, even chronic.

Finally, falling off to sleep may be easy since fatigue often turns to exhaustion in the early evening. But many persons suffering from excess adrenal stress waken in the middle of the night with too much energy and find it difficult to fall asleep again. This happens because continued adrenal gland stress results in excess cortisol production.

As with other problems, correction first involves finding the origin. Although many forms of therapy may help remedy the symptoms, the real cause may linger unless it is dealt with. After all, a symptom is just evidence—you want to address the cause, not just treat the evidence.

If the busy lifestyle that may have created the original stress is not modified, problems can continually recur somewhere in the person's chemistry, as either the same set of symptoms or a gathering of new ones.

This is a typical scenario of a chemically injured person. It begins innocently enough with a busy schedule that chemically overtaxes an unsuspecting adrenal system. It continues by producing fatigue, hunger, irritability, and colds.

For some, however, this common primary chemical problem may lead to secondary structural symptoms; the cause may be different, but the structural symptoms will be much like those in the structural example above. Unfortunately, these end-result structural symptoms, secondary to the chemical stress, are often seen as the chief problem because they are most apparent. That is why many therapies don't work on a given individual: the real problem is never found, so the body cannot heal.

In less fortunate individuals the chemical injury may also trigger a mental impairment.

The Mental or Emotional Injury

When we think of mental problems, visions of psychological tension and long-term therapy come to mind. But we should distinguish the mental state from the psychological and realize that many athletes struggle with mental distress but are psychologically stable. If the brain becomes distorted because of the chemical effects of diet, nutrition, or training, a mental injury may result. The problem is not uncommon in people who exercise.

Not long ago "Robert" was in his third year of sheer athletic greatness. His training never felt better, and in a race he was nearly unbeatable. Always full of energy, and without injury, Robert was climbing the ladder to national success. But in recent months Robert has become more depressed. His anxiety is evident, as is his dread of competition. Not only has his desire to train diminished but his personal life is being affected as well.

There are several ways the brain can be injured in the absence of disease. A functional imbalance in the brain's chemistry—a subtle yet noticeable change in certain substances called *neurotransmitters*—can modify the way we think, feel, and act. Fortunately, with few exceptions, these problems are reversible and, more importantly, preventable.

These brain imbalances may be caused by a mismatched diet or by overtraining. Let's look at what may have happened to Robert in the months before his mental injury. But first, a quick look at how physical and chemical our mental state can be.

Normally, when we think a thought or perceive a sensation from the outside world, it's the result of major chemical reactions in our brain. Billions of messages are sent throughout the brain and body on a regular basis because of chemicals called *neurotransmitters*. The neurotransmitters in our brain make us feel certain ways— high, low, sleepy, awake, happy, sad. Sometimes the brain may have too much of one type of chemical or not enough of another. As a result, we may feel too high or too low, agitated or depressed.

Most of the 35 or more neurotransmitters are made from amino acids derived from dietary protein and often influenced by the amount of dietary carbohydrates via the hormone insulin. Two important neurotransmitters are serotonin and norepinephrine.

Serotonin is produced with the help of the amino acid tryptophan and requires the hormone insulin. This neurotransmitter has a calming, sedating, or depressing effect. Eating a high-carbohydrate meal such as pasta or oatmeal or eating sweets results in more serotonin production. So the individual who is overactive may benefit from a high-carbohydrate meal, but that same meal might make an individual who is already a bit low feel worse, even to the point of depression. Sweets are traditionally thought of as providing energy, but in actuality they have a sedating effect. (At first sweets may seem to make us more alert, but that feeling is very short-lived.) In Robert's case, the overproduction of serotonin—a common problem even in athletes—helped establish his mental injury.

Norepinephrine is produced with the help of the amino acid tyrosine when little or no insulin is present. A high-protein meal with little or no carbohydrates will provide the brain with increased norepinephrine levels. This neurotransmitter has a stimulating effect on the brain. Often, the person who needs a pickup or is depressed could benefit from more of this brain chemical.

An imbalance in serotonin and norepinephrine, with a shift toward the former, may produce certain types of depression. Perhaps Robert was eating too many sweets and other carbohydrates. Let's look at the therapeutic options available to him.

Certain drugs are sometimes recommended for patients with chemical imbalances because they can manipulate brain chemistry and possibly create a better balance between neurotransmitters. The depressed athlete may be given medication to enhance or block certain neurotransmitters. Prozac, Elavil, and Tofranil are examples of antidepressants that affect the balance of serotonin and norepinephrine, thereby changing the way we feel. (Tranquilizers, such as Valium and Ativan, function in other ways through different neurotransmitters.)

Fortunately, most people do not need medication. But if you are overactive or depressed, you may benefit from simply altering your diet to modify your brain chemistry in the most appropriate way. In Robert's case, decreasing his intake of sugar and other carbohydrates and increasing his intake of protein foods may be very effective.

Robert's training also may have contributed to his mental injury, especially if he was overtrained. Overtraining can put stress on the nervous system and lead to emotional instability.

Overtraining frequently is preceded by too much anaerobic exercise. Although you are probably familiar with the relationship between lactic acid and anaerobic exercise, you may not be aware of lactic acid's effect on the mental state. For a long time scientists have known that increased lactic acid from anaerobic muscles converts to lactate in the blood, which may provoke depression, anxiety, and phobias.

It has even been shown that infusion of lactate into relatively normal subjects produces anxiety, depression, and panic. Given this, perhaps Robert's training and racing resulted in the production of too much lactic acid.

Fortunately, Robert can get out of his crisis. Although it's not impossible for him to do it alone, it would probably be easier with the help of a friend, family member, or professional. Whatever the case, it's important to look at the whole picture.

The big picture includes what happened at the onset. Was Robert training beyond his ability? Was he racing too much, or was he eating the wrong foods? More than likely, it was a combination of things. Sitting down and assessing each aspect of his life would be a good first step for Robert. Being objective is the hard part, and that's where others can help. Accepting that there really is a problem may also be a difficult hill to climb.

Making the appropriate changes, whatever they may be, can often result in a speedy remedy. Within a couple of weeks, perhaps sooner, Robert can be feeling better and those around him will be able to see the difference.

Physical injuries are common, but they are not the only type. They may be due to physical problems, but often they are secondary to chemical problems. And chemical injuries may be more common than physical ones. In addition, mental/emotional injuries can occur in people who are out of balance, often as a result of improper exercise.

Mending Your Own Injury

"The doctor who treats himself has a fool for a patient."

I recall that comment from my later years in school. The same holds true for anyone with an injury. It's very difficult to be as objective about your own ills as someone else can be.

At the same time, I've encountered countless patients who sought care for simple injuries but could not be helped. Although there are many good doctors and therapists around, there are many more incompetent ones. Overall, I think people must take responsibility for their own bodies. This may include getting help from a professional, but it always involves some degree of helping yourself.

When you're injured or when you sense the functional problems that precede a more obvious injury, you should seek the help of a professional— a physician, a massage therapist, a physical therapist. As long as your problem is corrected—that is, as long as the *cause* of your problem is corrected—with no side effects, the method you choose is not important.

Often I am asked, "What can I do for my ———?" You fill in the blank: ilio-tibial band syndrome, knee problem, back pain. The list is long. Physical injuries can become epidemic in those who exercise. The main reason is usually overtraining. By far the best way to solve this chronic problem is to prevent these injuries. But that advice doesn't help the thousands, probably millions, who are presently afflicted with some injury.

The most effective way to both prevent injuries and "treat" those that already exist is to build a solid aerobic base. In addition, here are more important concepts to consider:

You, and not the name of your injury, should be the focus of your therapy. There's no cookbook cure for ilio-tibial band syndrome or lower-back pain. The reality is that everyone's ITB problem is different. So from the start forget about the name since it's often not accurate. (Exceptions include situations that involve medical emergencies, such as a fracture, ruptured tendon, or other serious problem.) Don't let the doctor or other practitioner speculate on what you may have, trying to attach a name to your symptoms. Instead, find out what the problem is or is not. And find out what you can do to help your body correct its own problems. After all, that's what it's supposed to do. Generally speaking, most injuries are not serious. However, if they are not corrected and continue to prevent you from training, they may become more serious and adversely affect your quality of life.

Most injuries are functional rather than pathological. A functional problem is like a car's not starting: there's a relatively minor problem that can be easily corrected by the right mechanic.

A pathological problem is comparable to needing a new engine, or a new car: the problem is often very serious and not completely reversible. A broken bone, a tumor, or an injury that can only be corrected by a surgical procedure is a pathological problem. In gen-

The Correct Therapy

Randy was a high-school football player who had pain in both knees, including just below the patella (kneecap). During activity the pain was nearly debilitating, so the season seemed to be over for Randy. Despite relatively normal X rays, Randy's pediatrician diagnosed Randy's problem as Osgood-Schlatter's disease. When his doctor offered no therapy other than to stop playing, Randy consulted me. I found a number of imbalances in muscles that support the knees and ankles. Through a variety of conservative therapies during two treatment sessions, these imbalances were corrected. This eliminated the pain, and Randy could walk comfortably without difficulty. After another week he was able to return to working out without any recurrent problems, and he was able to play during the remainder of the season without any knee problems.

eral, these conditions require radical rather than conservative treatment. Fortunately, these pathological problems are not common. Unfortunately, many athletes and professionals use words that describe a pathological problem to describe an injury that is simply functional.

Functional problems are often soft-tissue injuries, from simple muscle imbalances to minor ligament or tendon strain or sprain. Even though these injuries usually are not serious, they can be very painful and even debilitating. In contrast to pathological injuries, functional problems are usually correctable with conservative measures and completely reversible. This can be accomplished by a doctor or other therapist or quite often by the person who has them. It is ideal to find a professional who can evaluate and treat these problems, but too often these caregivers are not successful, leaving the job to you.

So what can you do to help correct your own injury? Here are some general suggestions that have proved successful over time.

The Maffetone Method

Don't underestimate their effectiveness because of simplicity: most injuries have simple remedies.

▶ Find an activity that does not aggravate the problem and do it. There's nothing worse than being on a program and having to stop. This reduction or lack of exercise could become an aggravating factor. Walking is a great remedy if it doesn't hurt. Running in a pool is also good. Four feet of water will provide some but not too much gravity stress, which can actually help many injuries. Stationary equipment sometimes works well too. Try to spend the same amount of time doing these activities (or combinations) as you would spend on your normal workout.

▶ If pain accompanies your injury, let it guide you. If the pain improves as your workout progresses, that's generally a good sign. If the pain isn't exacerbated following the activity, that's even better. But if the pain gets worse with your activity, stop immediately. Either try another activity or wait a couple of days and try to work out again, following the rules below.

• Make sure you warm up properly before all your activities. Both warming up and cooling down have a therapeutic effect on your whole body, from your muscles to your metabolism. In many cases, lengthening both your warm-up and your cooldown can also help significantly. For many people, the best rehabilitation is a workout made up of only a warm-up and a cooldown.

• Avoid stretching. Many injuries are the result of over-stretched muscles, with tightness developing as a secondary problem.

• Keep all your workouts strictly aerobic until your injury heals. Do not attempt any anaerobic training until you have been symptom-free for at least a month or more, especially considering you may need to build an aerobic base.

• Be even more conservative with your maximum aerobic heart rate. You may find that training at 10 or 15 bpm below your maximum aerobic heart rate will be pain-free, whereas you may feel pain if you work at your maximum rate.

- *No matter what type of exercise you perform, take a good look at your shoes. The shoes, sandals, and other footwear that you wear throughout the day may cause problems.*
- *Plan your rehabilitation process. Don't be taken in by the idea that you need to "work through the pain." Begin your rehabilitation by taking three to five days off. Ideally this should occur when an injury is in the early stages, before it becomes extreme. This gives the body a chance to recover and possibly correct its own problems.*

The most important aspect of an injury is that it can teach you something about your body, your training, or your equipment. That will make you more immune to injuries, and your exercise will be more efficient.

17

The Diaphragm Muscle

Of all the vital muscles necessary for optimal performance, perhaps the most important one is the diaphragm muscle. This large, flat muscle allows us to breathe; it pulls in oxygenated air and, more important, expels unwanted carbon dioxide.

The Diaphragm and the Abdominals

An important relationship exists between the diaphragm and the abdominal muscles. Our culture has produced an attitude that makes us overly anxious about our abdomens. Most people think a flat, hard belly is ideal. And many people achieve this through endless sit-ups, crunches, and other ab exercises. But abdominal muscles that are too tight can inhibit the functioning of the diaphragm, adversely affecting oxygen intake and carbon dioxide removal. This is a common problem in many people who exercise, whereas most people don't want the high-powered, steel-like abdominals of body builders. It's much more important to improve the function of the diaphragm muscle.

Disturbing the balance between the diaphragm and the abdominal muscles could affect the body's entire structure—the lower back, the neck, the shoulders, even other areas such as the hips and knees. In addition, the intake of oxygen and the removal of carbon dioxide can influence body chemistry, especially the delicate acid and alkaline balance (pH). And certainly our mental state can be adversely affected when our physical or chemical body is not functioning properly.

One result of disturbing the delicate balance between the diaphragm and the abdominal muscles can be a change in the way you breathe. Let's first consider the normal breathing mechanism:

1. *During inhalation the abdominal muscles relax and are gently pushed out, allowing the diaphragm muscle to contract and fall. There is also a simultaneous but slight extension of the spine.*

2. *Exhalation involves the mild contracting (tightening), or pulling in, of the abdominal muscles accompanied by a slight flexion of the spine.*

3. *The chest should not be a major player during normal breathing. It should expand significantly only during more forced inhalation, and only after the abdominals have relaxed (i.e., are pushed out).*

During a hard workout or during competition additional expansion of the lungs is necessary. In this case the chest is expanded greatly during inhalation, but only after the abdominals have relaxed and the diaphragm has contracted.

This sounds easy enough, but many people breathe just the opposite way: they pull their abdomen in when inhaling and expand their chest. As a result, less air and oxygen is taken into the lungs and less carbon dioxide is removed. This can be a cumulative stress on your entire body over time. This incorrect breathing style is often the result of social stress; people tend to hold the abdomen tense, and they don't want the belly to appear too big. "Stomach in, chest out!" my gym teacher used to yell.

Sit quietly and think about your breathing. Are you doing it correctly? If you're breathing improperly, you must first relearn the normal mechanism. Stand with one hand on the mid- to lower abdomen and one hand on the lower spine, and slowly practice breathing in and out. Think of the area where your hands are as a vessel that you are attempting to fill with air.

Another method of training the diaphragm muscle is the straw exercise. This method, which helps improve the *power* of the diaphragm muscle, involves breathing deeply, and slowly, in and out of a straw. At first you may only be able to do this for a few seconds, but then work your way up to a minute or more. Work up to several sets of one minute each, three times a week, for 8 to 10 weeks. This may be very difficult at first if you have a weak diaphragm, but soon you will have no trouble.

There are some simple tests you or a professional can perform to measure your diaphragm function:

- *Vital capacity is a good measure of lung capacity and general diaphragm function. Vital capacity is related to physiological age: the lower the vital capacity, the older you are physiologically, and vice versa.*

- *A simple test you can do yourself is to measure* breath-holding time. *This measures the general capacity of the diaphragm and lung volume. Take a deep breath and see how long you can hold it. Anyone in good health should be able to hold his or her breath for at least 50–60 seconds.*

- *Another test related to the diaphragm is Snider's Test, which measures the strength of the diaphragm using the power in the breath. Hold a small lit match six inches away from your mouth. With your mouth wide open, try to blow the match out. You should be able to do this easily. Be careful not to ignite your hair.*

Breathing in Step

Another important aspect of breathing has to do with its relationship to workout movements. Specifically, if you're running, jogging, or walking, it's common to breathe in for two, three, or four steps and exhale for about the same number. This may result in always inhaling when your right foot hits the ground, for example. Since the whole body physically responds to the act of breathing—the abdominal movement, spinal flexion and extension, and so on—you should make sure that the same phase of breathing is not always associated with the same gait. This can be accomplished by varying how long you breathe in and out:

1. *While running, inhale for the duration of two steps.*

2. *Exhale for the duration of three steps.*

Using this method, you will reduce the physical stress placed on any one joint; for example, you won't always be inhaling when your right foot strikes the ground. Making your exhalation last one step longer than your inhalation forces you to remove more carbon dioxide.

If you're jogging slowly, you may breathe in a "three in–four out" pattern. For example,

1. *Inhale for the duration of three steps.*

2. *Exhale for the duration of four steps.*

Any pattern may be useful; for example, a four-in-five out pattern is common during walking. A one-in-two out pattern may be used when running anaerobically, especially during a race. Following a pattern forces you to focus on your breathing, especially the normal movement of the abdominal muscles. This will also result in toning the abdominal muscles without the anaerobic sit-ups and crunches so commonly recommended (which commonly cause lower-back stress).

You can apply this movement to cycling, step machines, aerobic dance, and any other type of workout. When swimming, it's important to turn your head both ways during the breathing process. Many people have developed the bad habit of only turning to their right side when swimming laps. It's worth taking the time to retrain yourself to turn your head to both sides to breathe and to maintain balance and normal gait.

Breathing is the most important motion your body goes through, one that provides you with continuous benefits. If your breathing action is altered, through bad habits, for example, your whole body can be adversely affected. You may need to train yourself to breathe correctly. To be sure that your diaphragm muscle is functioning properly, test yourself: perform the breath-holding test or even Snider's test or check your vital capacity.

18

If Einstein Were Your Coach

> Whether you're just beginning an exercise program, in a rehabilitation program, or training to run a marathon, Albert Einstein would say that one key to an effective program is taking charge of the time element.

Einstein said, "Time is relative." He postulated that a spacecraft leaving earth and traveling at nearly the speed of light for 20 years would return to earth with a different record of time elapsed than that on earth. If you compared two identical clocks—one on the spacecraft and one on earth—the clock on the spacecraft might show that 10 years had elapsed, but the clock on earth would show that 20 years had passed. Moreover, the passengers on the spacecraft would have aged only 10 years, while those on earth would have aged 20 years. This idea of "two clocks" providing us with different times for the same event can be useful. Let's see how we can relate it to exercise.

We know that in a given situation the human body can sense and react to time differently. A good movie passes quickly, while a boring one lasts forever. In my practice I've observed that the relativity of time is certainly something to reckon with in exercise. This is as true for beginners as it is for those in competition. "Time is not a constant thing by any means," says Olympic marathoner Lorraine Moller, of New Zealand. "When you're in a good race, everything comes together. Time flies when you're having fun."

Time can be experienced as a nonflowing, isolated part of any workout. This view of time is most evident when we're falling in love, meditating, or in a trance. As Dr. Larry Dossey, M.D., states in his book *Space, Time, and Medicine*, "These experiences suggest that an alternative to the ordinary means of experiencing time lies

---

Bad Timing

Jennifer was fatigued, increasingly overweight, and feeling older than her 42 years. After evaluating her, I recommended that she begin an easy aerobic exercise for 15 minutes daily. Jennifer chose to ride a stationary bike that had been in her room, used only as a clothes tree. But Jennifer's first attempt was a disaster: 15 minutes seemed like an hour, and an hour was just too much, not just mentally but chemically and physically as well.

Tim had been running regularly for five years, and at age 37 he was training for his fourth marathon. He was hoping to break the elusive 3-hour barrier since he'd come close twice before. His training schedule included the traditional "long" Sunday run of 2 hours, and he would soon increase it to 2.5 hours. However, relative to even his "longest" run, how long would the 3-hour marathon seem to Tim? In other words, if for Tim 2 hours was long and 2.5 hours was the longest, was 3 hours reasonable? Tim needed to modify his approach or he'd fail to attain his goal, as so many do in events that have a significant time factor. Both psychologically and physiologically he had to come to see 3 hours as a "short" time.

---

within all of us." In our fast-paced society we tend to put time in a very short frame. Relative to that, everything else we do may be distorted, including our exercise time slot.

The cases of Jennifer and Tim are common examples of people for whom time is a problem in their exercise program. The remedy is something Albert Einstein could provide.

Einstein was able to understand and relate to complex issues, but how could he help Jennifer and Tim, or anyone else, in their relatively simple quests? Using our earlier notion that a single event can be measured on two clocks will help anyone to control time more effectively.

Jennifer was comparing the time period of 15 minutes on the bike (first clock) to an hour (second clock). Thus, her inseparable body and mind responded to an hour rather than to 15 minutes. As a beginner, she wasn't able to start an exercise program with an hour of exercise. In addition, because it wasn't fun at all, Jennifer also viewed the time exercising as time lost (the "what-else-could-I-be-doing" syndrome), which increased her stress.

"A lot of coping with time," Lorraine Moller says, "is just learning to relax." Jennifer's inability to cope with two "clocks" that were reading two different "times" was the problem, and this had to be changed.

I gradually moved Jennifer's clocks closer together by decreasing her time on the bike in one- or two-minute increments until she reached the point when she felt that both clocks were the same. That important starting point turned out to be four minutes; it was relaxing and gave her a feeling of accomplishment. But she wondered whether only four minutes of exercise was worth it. I explained that she'd never benefit, or at best would always struggle on her program, unless she found the right starting point, one at which both clocks were the same. As the weeks went by, Jennifer was able to increase her time on the bike gradually, until after three months she was exercising for 45 minutes five days a week and really enjoying it. Now Jennifer's energy is high and, with three inches off her waist, she feels young again.

Tim also had a problem with two clocks. He wanted his "marathon clock" to read less time than the observed time: he wanted 3 hours to feel more like 1 hour. One of Tim's problems was that he was using his "longest" run to train for an event that would take more time than the training run. In other words, the marathon was even longer than his "longest" run. Tim had to experience a workout of more than 3 hours, without overtraining, so that the marathon would be relatively shorter. He also had to learn how to manipulate time at will.

Walking was one remedy for both of these time problems. By adding more time to his weekly long run, by walking a half-hour before and after his run, Tim could increase the total time of his long training session without risking running too much, a problem he had had in the past. Walking also relaxed him in a way that running never did. After two or three of these workouts, Tim learned how easy it was to manipulate time. His total workout of 3.5 hours—a half-hour walk followed by a 2.5-hour run and then another half-hour walk—enabled him to make the time go "faster" or, now that he didn't want the new, more enjoyable workout to end, "slower." These workouts would re-orient Tim, making the marathon shorter relative to the long workout. On marathon day he would be able to make the marathon go by quickly. Which is exactly what happened: Tim ran his race in 2 hours and 48 minutes, and afterwards he said that "it felt like an easy long run."

I used these same physiological and psychological factors to train Paul Fendler, who, in his first-ever ultra-marathon distance, became the New York Metropolitan Athletic Congress 50-Mile Champion in 1987. "All of a sudden, in the beginning of the race, time ceased to be an existing factor," Fendler recalls, "and it was the walk/run workouts that taught me how to control time."

Jennifer's friend Jane had another common problem that distorts the physiology. Jane became lost in her novel while riding a stationary bike at the health club for 30 minutes. She said, "It's like five minutes, the time goes so fast."

Relative Time

If Einstein were her coach, he might say that she really wasn't getting 30 minutes of exercise even though she was riding the bike for 30 minutes. Because she had succeeded in making the time go "fast," she was getting less out of a workout according to her other clock. And, indeed, this is what seemed to happen. After seven months of exercise Jane hadn't benefited very much. It was as if she had done nothing. I changed Jane's view of time by having her stop reading so that she felt 30 minutes go by, and after a few weeks her clothing sizes began to decrease and she had more energy. This doesn't mean that your workout needs to feel so long that it's boring. When properly done, exercise should be enjoyable and give you a feeling of accomplishment.

If at the end of the 30-minute workout (or however long your workout is) you feel that 30 minutes have passed, you're doing fine. But if after 30 minutes it feels like only 5 or 10 minutes have gone by, then perhaps your benefits will be more like the benefits you might derive from 5 or 10 minutes of exercise. In such a case it's quite possible that you may not reach your exercise goals. To correct this problem, you may need to adjust your exercise time until both "clocks" measure 30 minutes. On the other hand, if after 30 minutes of exercise you feel that an hour has gone by, perhaps you're overexercising.

Einstein thought in holistic terms and believed that no activity in the universe was random. This certainly would include the organization of the human body and the influence of many factors that affect exercise habits. "Time" is merely one of them.

19

Training Schedules
for Competition

Training for both health and fitness involves
a number of factors: experience, technique, intuition, and some basic knowledge about the body. And if you decide
to compete, there are some fundamental
things you need to consider regarding your
training schedule. By far the most important consideration is this: You need first to
understand the primary rules of exercise as
described in this book—warming up, cooling down, exercising at your target heart
rate, and so on—and successfully apply
them. If you do that, your daily schedule
will become secondary. Exactly how many
minutes per day you train will no longer be
the main focus. Your schedule will fall into
place on its own.

Perhaps a better title for this chapter would be "Less Is More"
since for the average person who wishes to compete but has many
other responsibilities, such as work, family responsibilities, and so
on, less training usually produces better athletic performance.

Trying to accumulate many hours of training usually means squeezing workouts into an already hectic day.

The majority of the athletes I have worked with in my career, like most of the readers of this book, are not professionals. If you have a full-time job and perhaps a family, a house, and other responsibilities, you can still train and compete at a very high level. But don't expect to be able to put in the same amount of time and miles as professional athletes. Nor do you need to in order to succeed.

Most of the time, I find that decreasing the total training hours per week allows for more recovery and results in less stress. This helps you build a much more efficient aerobic system. When race season comes, you'll be more refreshed and ready to race.

The majority of the benefits received from training occur in the first 10 weeks of the season. You can very easily maintain these benefits during the rest of the season with much less training. Studies show that this can be done by cutting training by two-thirds! If you

A Marked Improvement

Carla was a back-of-the-pack triathlete with hopes of improving her performance. But after her fourth year of diminishing returns, she sought help with her schedule. While Carla was doing all the right things—warming up and cooling down, not exceeding her maximum aerobic heart rate, and other routines, her workout schedule averaged 18 hours per week. Unfortunately, Carla really didn't have the time for that amount of training, but she tried to squeeze in the workouts. She worked part-time and had a family that included two young children.

In mid-November I recommended that she cut her workout schedule to about 12 hours per week. It was the only change necessary. In next summer's racing season she achieved personal bests in eight out of nine races. Carla also placed in the top five of her age group in half of those events, a feat she had never accomplished before.

train regularly, year after year, your rate of improvement will be slower in the later years, but you can maintain that improvement with much less effort. Additional effort will not necessarily produce more improvements.

Other studies show no evidence that in single-sport activities multiple daily training sessions will improve performance more than single daily sessions. For example, a study of two groups of swimmers, one training twice daily and one training only once a day, demonstrated no difference in the heart rate and lactate levels or performance times of the two groups. Another study measured the performance of swimmers over a five-year period and showed no difference in the performance of those who swam 10,000 meters daily and those who swam half that distance daily.

Despite the evidence that less training offers the same or increased benefits, endurance athletes still tend to overtrain. Part of the problem may be social.

Athletes today, especially in the United States, still subscribe to the "no pain, no gain" philosophy of exercise. This philosophy is reinforced in advertising, magazine articles, and schools. Very young athletes are exposed to this philosophy long before they learn about being healthy and fit. In many cases they learn about fitness after it's too late.

Learning about yourself—including your commitment, the amount of time you can allot to working out, your goals, and so on—will help you determine the schedule that is right for you. If you are training for a single sport, you'll have an easier schedule than you would have if you are a multisport athlete. Most of the time you'll have only one workout a day. The best time to do this depends on your daily nontraining schedule. Many runners, for example, find a morning workout most suitable. Other sports have limits: swimmers usually have pool hours to consider; cyclists and skiers are limited by the weather. I frequently recommend that single-sport athletes perform some other event one to three times per week. This *cross training* has a positive benefit, especially for the nervous system, as long as it is aerobic and fits into your schedule.

If you are a multisport athlete—such as a triathlete, who swims, bikes, and runs, or a duathlete, who bikes and runs—you'll have a busier training schedule. But you don't have to perform each sport every day.

One luxury of being a professional athlete is that it is your job to train and race. You can devote most, if not all, of the day to training. Not that you'd work out all day. A professional triathlete might swim for an hour in the morning, go for a two-hour bike ride at midday, and then run for an hour in the late afternoon. But if you're an age-group athlete (i.e., not a professional), this schedule usually won't work.

Individuals who engage in more than one sport often don't have time to work out in all their events each day. Nor is that required. However, many endurance athletes attempt this, sometimes no matter what the outcome.

Less Is More

Jay was stuck in an overtraining cycle for at least three years. He would train in each of his three events as many days as possible. He would run at 5:00 A.M., swim at noon, and ride late in the day. The problem was that Jay had his own business and worked from 7:00 A.M. until 9:00 P.M. He also had a family. Maintaining that type of training schedule five days a week, with Tuesdays and Thursdays reserved for his long bike ride and his long run, respectively, was quite a chore.

Jay would become exhausted regularly, and about every couple of months he'd have to take a week or two off because of fatigue or injury. As he started feeling better, he would pick up his "normal" schedule again. I helped Jay match his program to his needs, explaining how it would make him race better as well as improve his health. However, he could not understand how one could improve his race times without putting in the high-mileage weeks he was used to. Jay never returned to my office, but occasionally I would meet him at a race, where year after year he showed no improvement and always had some type of injury.

If you're a single-sport athlete and you want to add some cross training to your schedule, your week might look something like this:

▶ *Tuesday, Wednesday, Friday: run 45 minutes*

▶ *Sunday: run 60–75 minutes*

▶ *Monday and Thursday: ride the stationary bike 45 minutes*

▶ *Saturday: off*

If you're a multisport athlete and perform each activity at least three days a week, your schedule can be very effective. If you attempt to do otherwise, you risk overtraining. Try not to perform the same activity on consecutive days. For example,

▶ *Monday, Wednesday, Saturday: swim 45 minutes*

▶ *Tuesday, Thursday, Saturday, Sunday: bike 1–2 hours, depending on the weather*

▶ *Monday and Sunday: run 45 minutes*

▶ *Thursday: run 75 minutes*

For most athletes the weekend can provide time for longer workouts, such as a longer bike ride on Saturday and a longer run on Sunday. Or, you can combine two events to make one longer workout, such as a 2-hour bike ride followed by a 45-minute run. A favorite winter workout is a swim immediately followed by an hour of indoor biking. These combined sessions not only provide a longer workout but mimic race transitions, in which your body has to adjust to the stress of changing from one event to another.

Be sure to get at least one off day. If you feel better calling it a rest or recovery day, go right ahead. To some people the word *off* means not doing anything. But days off are an important part of the training formula. Remember, training = workout + rest.

I recommend at least one rest day per week to help with recovery. During the racing season, when you will more easily maintain your fitness level with less training but require more recovery, two rest days would be even better. Off days are best taken just before the weekend if the weekend is your busiest training time or if there is a race on the weekend. Another appropriate time is Monday, which is a day when you need to devote a lot of your energy to recovery. Or make Monday an easy day if Friday is your off day and the weekend includes a lot of training.

When planning rest days (and easy ones), consider your work stress too. If Monday is always your busiest or hardest day on the job, don't train that day.

Seasonal stress may also be a factor. If you're an accountant and your busiest time is tax season in the early spring, make that an easy training period and postpone your racing until early summer. Another important time to take it easy is at the end of your training and racing year. For most athletes this is November or December. At this time I recommend taking at least two to three weeks off. Periods of rest allow the body to recover not only physically but also mentally. During this time just let your body do what it wants: watch TV, go for hikes, paint your house. But don't do things that are strenuous if you're not used to it. For example, don't chop wood or build a stone wall if it's something you don't normally do.

At this point you may expect me to provide a training schedule. There is no schedule that would prove ideal for all the readers of this book. If you keep in mind all the rules—from warming up to exercising at the proper heart rate to cooling down—and fit your workouts into your week so that they won't add stress, you'll have no trouble formulating your own schedule. This is the approach I follow in my office—with age-group athletes as well as the pros.

20

Diet and Nutrition

This chapter briefly highlights how certain foods, nutrients, and eating habits help or hurt your ability to build an aerobic base, control stress, and burn more body fat.

General Dietary Recommendations

While dietary habits vary from person to person, there are some basic "dos and don'ts" for improving overall body function that everyone should consider:

Drink at least six 8-ounce glasses of water per day—between meals, not during meals. If you exercise more than about an hour a day, you may need ten, twelve, or more glasses of water. And if your protein intake is very high, for example, above 100 grams per day, then you will need much more water. Try not to drink water within 20 minutes before a meal and or within 90 minutes after. Avoid drinking water with meals; it may dilute your digestive enzymes, making digestion less efficient (and therefore resulting in poor absorption of nutrients). Our bodies are very dependent on outside sources of water. Coffee, tea, juices, and other liquids are not substitutes for water because the body processes them as foods, when what the body needs is water. Some liquids, such as coffee, tea, and soda, actually cause the body to lose water. One exception to drinking liquids with meals is wine, which can help the digestive process. But drink only what you enjoy and can tolerate, and no more than about two or three 4-ounce glasses, less if you are carbohydrate intolerant.

Avoid sugar and foods that contain sugar. This includes cakes, cookies, pies, soda, ketchup, cereals, and other foods to which large amounts of sugar have been added. Read the labels on the products you buy. Other names for sugar include sucrose, dextrose, lactose, maltose, and glucose. Corn syrup, maltodextrin, glucose polymers, and high-fructose corn syrup should be avoided. Even some artificial sweeteners, which should also be avoided, actually contain sugar.

Avoid all hydrogenated or partially hydrogenated oils and fats, fried foods, and fats or oils that may be rancid. Hydrogenated or partially hydrogenated oils interfere with the normal metabolism of fats. Hydrogenation is a process used in manufacturing such items as margarine, chips, crackers, and cookies. Foods containing palm and palm kernel oil should also be avoided; read labels to find out whether these oils have been used. Added carbohydrates *during* training or racing is OK since this sugar is used immediately for energy.

Avoid products made with white flour, such as most breads, rolls, pasta, and so on. Whole-grain products, such as 100 percent whole wheat bread, whole rye crackers, and whole grain cereals (without sugar), are healthier choices than the less nutritional refined products. The "germ" of the grain contains significant amounts of the nutrients found in these products. When white flour is processed, the valuable germ is removed. Whole grain products also have more fiber, which is important for good health.

Use sea salt in cooking and salting foods if you like salt and are not sensitive to sodium. Sea salt tastes like regular table salt but contains a better balance of minerals as well as many trace minerals that your body requires. We evolved from the salt ocean and still require many of the sea's vital minerals.

Chew your food well. The human physiology requires that food be chewed before it is swallowed. Chickens have a gizzard, which allows them to pick up food and swallow it whole. The way some people eat, you would think they had a gizzard too. Chewing does more than break the food into smaller pieces. It's the beginning of the very important first stage of chemical digestion, especially for carbohydrates. Chewing and mixing saliva with your food also triggers reactions in the brain, which sends messages to the rest of the body preparing it to process and utilize the food. Many digestion-related problems can be greatly improved, if not eliminated, by chewing food.

Meals should be eaten in a relaxed environment. This means not while working, getting the kids ready for school or arguing about money. Get away from your stress, get off your feet, and relax. This allows the digestive system to function most efficiently.

Eat at least four to six servings of cooked vegetables each day. Include a rainbow of colors, such as green (broccoli, spinach, green beans), orange and red (carrots, tomatoes, peppers), yellow or white (cauliflower, zucchini, squash, mushrooms), and purple (eggplant, cabbage). In addition to these cooked vegetables, eat at least one raw salad daily; this might contain leaf lettuce, carrots, red or yellow peppers (green peppers, like green tomatoes, limes, and most apples, are unripe), celery, and whatever foods your body craves. If you can't tolerate too much raw food, have small amounts with each meal. Avoid iceberg lettuce; it's harder to digest and offers fewer nutrients than the tastier varieties of leaf lettuce. Also avoid *raw* broccoli and cauliflower as they contain natural enzymes that may disrupt metabolism. A minute of steaming will destroy these enzymes, making these foods safe to eat.

Eat two servings of fruits per day if you can tolerate them (based on

> ## The Top Diet Dos and Don'ts
> - Drink at least six 8-ounce glasses of water per day
> - Avoid sugar
> - Avoid hydrogenated and partially hydrogenated oils
> - Avoid white-flour products
> - Use sea salt
> - Chew your food
> - Eat in a relaxed environment
> - Eat at least four servings of cooked vegetables per day
> - Eat two servings of fruits per day
> - Eat some raw food at each meal

your level of carbohydrate tolerance). Choose from the less sweet fruits first—grapefruit, berries (strawberries, blueberries, raspberries), melons, plums. Eat sweet fruits only occasionally—grapes, bananas, and dried fruits (raisins, prunes, figs).

Eat some raw food at each meal. When you eat a food or other substance that is not tolerated well by your body, the immune system goes on alert. One indicator of this natural defense is an increase in white blood cells, which help your body fight foreign invaders. It is not unusual for the white-blood-cell count to increase following a meal that's void of raw food. But eating some raw food first prevents the typical defense response by your body. For most people, it's best to have some raw food before each meal. Examples of raw additions include avocados, raw nuts, soft cooked eggs (raw yolk), and the traditional vegetables and fruits. Certain natural food supplements also contain foods not processed at high temperatures and can be considered "raw" since the enzymes have not been destroyed.

Carbohydrate Intolerance

One of the most common problems found in individuals who have a difficult time burning body fat is carbohydrate intolerance. This condition occurs in persons who eat more carbohydrate foods—breads, cereals, rice, potatoes, sugar and other sweets—than their body can properly metabolize. This results in the production of too much insulin, a hormone released by the pancreas. Too much insulin can prevent fat burning and cause you to store more and more fat in your body. Normally, about 40 percent of the carbohydrate foods you eat are converted to fat and stored. In many people this percentage is much higher due to excess insulin, the result of increased age, genetic predisposition, or stress. Many people whose diet contains 60–70 percent carbohydrates, or more, may be able to burn more fat and be healthier overall once they reduce their carbohydrate intake to a more tolerable level.

Here is a checklist that may help you determine your level of carbohydrate intolerance:

- *Do you get sleepy after meals?*

- *Do you experience bloating (intestinal) after meals?*

- *Do you find it difficult to concentrate after meals?*

- *Do you have, or is there a family history of, adult-onset diabetes, heart disease, or breast cancer?*

- *Do you have high blood pressure or a high cholesterol or triglyceride level?*

- *Do you need to snack frequently?*

- *Do you often have feelings of depression?*

- *Are you addicted to sweets, cigarettes, caffeine, or other substances?*

Even two or three "yes" answers may indicate that you are carbohydrate intolerant and eating a diet too high in carbohydrates.

The Two-Week Test

If you suspect that your carbohydrate intake is too high, consider taking the Two-Week Test. This self-evaluation can help you in two ways: first, it will help you decide whether you have a carbohydrate intolerance; and second, if you do, it will start you on the right path to finding your optimal level of carbohydrate intake.

The Two-Week Test provides you with a period of time in which your insulin levels remain relatively low because your carbohydrate intake is decreased.

Before you start the test, look at your answers to the questions in the above list. After the test, determine whether some or many of your complaints have changed. In addition, if you are concerned about your weight, weigh yourself before and after the test. (This is the only instance when I recommend using a scale.)

For a period of two weeks, do not eat any of the foods identified below as foods to avoid.

Foods to Avoid

Don't worry if these foods make up most of your diet. You'll have others (below) to replace them.

- bread, rolls, pasta, pancakes, cereal, muffins, rice cakes
- sweets, including products that contain sugar, such as ketchup, honey, and many other prepared foods (read the labels)
- fruits and fruit juices
- potatoes (all types), corn, rice, beans
- milk, half-and-half, yogurt
- so-called healthful snacks, such as 40-30-30 bars and sports drinks

Foods to Eat

You may eat as much of the following foods as you like.

- whole eggs, all real cheeses, cream
- all meats (beef, turkey, lamb, etc.), but beware: many cold cuts are cured in sugar and should be avoided
- all fish and shellfish
- tomato, V-8, and other vegetable juices (such as carrot)
- all vegetables (except potatoes, beans, and corn), cooked or raw, and tofu
- nuts, seeds, nut butters
- oils, vinegar, mayonnaise, mustard, butter (but no hydrogenated oils)
- sea salt is highly recommended unless you are sensitive to sodium

Before you start the test, make sure you have enough of the foods you'll be eating during the test. And get rid of any sweets in your house so that you won't be tempted.

Do not allow yourself to get hungry. Eating five or six small meals is preferable to eating two or three large ones. Eat as many eggs, as much cheese or meat, and as many vegetables as you need to avoid hunger. Remember, this test will only last two weeks. You will not be eating like this forever. Don't worry about cholesterol, fat, calories, or the amount of food you're eating.

The test should not be difficult, although it will probably represent a big change from the way you've been eating. Many people with carbohydrate intolerance have been eating a high-carbohydrate, low-fat and low-protein diet. If you've been eating lots of sweets or other carbohydrates, you may experience cravings for sugar (sometimes referred to as carbohydrate addiction) for a few days during the test. Eat something on the acceptable list instead and stick it out. Doing the test with a friend is very helpful. Doing it with several people is even better, as there will always be someone to talk to if your cravings become difficult to control (it's like quitting smoking).

Following the diet for less than two weeks probably will not give you a valid result. So, if after five days, for example, you eat a bowl of pasta or a bag of cookies, you will need to begin again.

After the Two-Week Test, look again at your list of complaints: Do you feel better now than you did two weeks ago? Did you lose weight? If nothing improved, then you may not be carbohydrate intolerant. If you do feel better—some say they feel like a new person—especially if you've lost weight (which would be from both fat and water weight), it is likely that you have some degree of carbohydrate intolerance and you've been eating too much carbohydrate food.

If the Two-Week Test improved your symptoms, the next step is to determine how much carbohydrate food you can tolerate without a recurrence of any of those symptoms.

Begin by adding *small* amounts of carbohydrates to your diet, such as a slice of bread at lunch or half of a potato with dinner. Whatever you add, make sure it's not a refined carbohydrate: no foods containing sugar or refined flour (e.g., white bread, rolls, or pasta), brown rice instead of white.

Don't add a carbohydrate to two meals in a row. Because the

amount of insulin production is partly based on your previous meal, add a carbohydrate at *every other* meal or snack.

Every time you add carbohydrates, watch for any of the symptoms that were eliminated by the test. Be on the lookout especially for symptoms that develop immediately after eating, such as intestinal bloating, sleepiness after meals, or depression. If your hunger or craving disappeared during the two weeks and now has returned, you've probably eaten too many carbohydrates. If you lost 8 pounds during the test and have gained back 5 after adding some carbohydrates for a week or two, you've probably eaten too many carbohydrates.

During the Two-Week Test and forever after be sure to drink lots of water. Most people need at least 6 to 10 eight-ounce glasses per day. Generally, the more protein you consume, the more water you need between meals.

The Importance of Snacking to Burn Fat

Blood sugar stress is commonly associated with carbohydrate intolerance (and often associated with adrenal stress as well). This stress can be avoided by eating every two to three hours. This is why studies have shown that eating small meals between the major meals can help you burn more fat and reduce weight. These between-meal "snacks," however, must contain healthful food—only real food and real food products. Avoid margarine and highly processed food.

When snacking, as at all other meals, it's important to avoid the following processed food items:

- *Sugars: maltodextrin, glucose polymers, corn syrup, high-fructose corn syrup, barley malt or maltose.*

- *Proteins: all predigested protein, hydrolyzed proteins, and all protein isolates and caseinates containing monosodium glutamate (MSG).*

- **Oils and fats:** *all fractionated oils, palm and palm kernel oils, and hydrogenated oils, as well as foods high in saturated fats.*

- **All artificial ingredients:** *artificial flavors, sweeteners, colors, etc., including synthetic vitamins, which are prominent in many processed foods. Foods containing nutrients such as thiamine hydrochloride, magnesium oxide, and ascorbic acid or nutrients described as equivalent to 100 percent or 50 percent of daily values (DV) are synthetic.*

Avoid snacks that are high in carbohydrates just before working out and especially before competitive endurance races. Eating food containing too many carbohydrates before exercise can reduce your

Follow the Plan

Bob was determined to renew his health in a natural way. He was overweight and overfat, exhausted all the time, and his blood pressure, cholesterol, and triglycerides were too high. He took the Two-Week Test and initially felt very good. But within a few days he began to get tired and irritable. After talking with Bob for just a few minutes, I realized that he was doing several things wrong. Because he had to spend more time in bathrooms, he did not drink much water during the day. And when he thought about how many calories he was eating, he became calorie-conscious and ate less. To make matters worse, he thought that yogurt was in the cheese group and was eating two or three containers of fruit yogurt each day. When I told Bob that each container of yogurt contained 6–7 teaspoons of sugar and to forget about the calories for now and force the water, he started his test again. After the first week he was feeling great. Within a month his energy was being maintained, his blood pressure, cholesterol, and triglyceride levels returned to normal, and he lost 14 pounds.

body's ability to burn fat and increase its reliance on sugar. This can make you use up your glycogen stores more quickly, leading to earlier fatigue and reduced endurance. Eating or drinking *during* exercise does not cause insulin release.

Balancing Dietary Fat

To many people, *fats* is a four-letter word. However, the *good* dietary fats can help you get healthy and burn more body fat. The benefits of fat are in fact many!

Your aerobic system burns fat for energy and prevents excessive dependency on sugar, especially blood sugar. Your body is capable of obtaining as much as 80 to 90 percent of its energy from fat if you program your fat-burning mechanism. Fats provide more than twice as much potential energy as carbohydrates do (9 kilocalories compared with only 4 kilocalories of potential energy). The body even uses fats as a source of energy for heart muscle function; these fats, called *phospholipids*, normally are contained in the heart muscle and generate energy to make it work more efficiently.

Fats help our body make hormones that develop and maintain our health and life itself. But for the hormonal system to do its work properly, it must be able to make the appropriate hormones; many glands are dependent on fat for their production of hormones, such as the adrenal gland discussed earlier.

Hormone-like substances called *prostaglandins* (PGs), along with other natural chemicals necessary for such normal cell functions as inflammation, water balance, and circulation, are produced from dietary fats. PGs also act as messengers and control many other body functions. Depending on the balance of prostaglandins, we age more quickly or more slowly. These substances only survive for less than a second in the body, but they help us recover from injury and from the normal wear and tear of everyday living. The PGs (along with certain fats) also help regulate free radicals, which have been implicated in many disease states, from cancer to heart disease.

Fat is an insulator. The body's ability to store fat permits humans to live in most climates, especially in areas of extreme heat or cold. In warmer areas of the world stored fat provides protection from the heat; in colder lands increased fat storage beneath the skin prevents too much heat from leaving the body. An example of fat's effectiveness as an insulator is the Eskimos' ability to withstand great cold and remain in good health. The Eskimos' diet is high in omega-3 fats, and much of the fat they eat is stored under the skin. Moreover, Eskimos have a very low incidence of heart and other disease. Cholesterol also serves as an insulating barrier within the skin. Without this protection, water and water soluble substances such as chemical pollutants would enter the body through the skin. It's the protective qualities of fat that give the skin the soft, smooth, unwrinkled appearance so many people try to achieve through expensive skin conditioners. The healthy look of skin comes from the fat inside. The same is true for your hair. The proper balance and amount of fats in your diet will give your skin and hair a healthy appearance. In fact, if you've been looking for the ideal skin and hair product, you can end your search by balancing the fats in your diet.

Fat is important during pregnancy and lactation. For many years doctors told women not to gain too much weight during pregnancy—15, 20, or 25 pounds at most. Many women followed this advice by eliminating fats from their diet, which created nutritional deficiencies and problems with fat metabolism. This was unhealthy for both mother and baby. Today more doctors recommend a higher average weight gain during pregnancy. Depending on the woman's frame and her health, a weight gain of 30 or more pounds is considered acceptable. This change has been shown to result in healthier babies and mothers as long as the mother was active in the months after birth. Following birth, breast-feeding helps protect the baby against allergies, asthma, and intestinal problems because of the high-quality fat, especially cholesterol, contained in breast milk. Especially during the first few days, the baby is highly dependent on milk's fat for survival. During this time it is colostrum, the fatty component of milk, that benefits the baby most. This substance is of vital nutritional importance and one that has never been duplicated in artificial formulas.

Fats seem to help protect the body against the harmful effects of x-rays by physically protecting the cells and by controlling the production of free radicals that results from exposure to x-rays. In addition to medical x-rays, we are exposed to x-rays from the atmosphere all the time. This cosmic radiation penetrates most objects, including airplanes. The average person is exposed to more cosmic radiation during a flight from New York to Los Angeles than during all the medical x-rays he or she experiences throughout life.

Because so many people digest their food poorly (a common result of stress), they do not always efficiently absorb the nutrients in foods. You can be on the best diet in the world, but it's all a waste if you can't digest and absorb it properly. Lipase and bile are fatty substances that aid in the digestion and absorption of fats and fat-soluble vitamins. Fats also help regulate the rate at which the stomach empties. Fats slow the rate at which the stomach empties, allowing for better digestion of proteins. If you are always hungry, it may be because your meals are too low in fats and your stomach empties too rapidly. Fats also slow the absorption of sugar from the small intestines, which keeps insulin levels from rising too high and too quickly.

Fats offer physical support and protection to vital body parts, including the organs and glands. Fats act like a natural, built-in shock absorber, cushioning us from the wear and tear of everyday life. Fats help prevent organs from sinking in response to the downward pull of gravity. Fats also protect the inner lining of the stomach and intestines from irritating substances in the diet, such as alcohol and spicy foods.

Certain fats—cholesterol, for example—are important for vitamin D production through our skin in the reaction with the sun. This newly formed vitamin D is then absorbed into the blood, allowing calcium and phosphorous to be properly absorbed from the intestinal tract. Without vitamin D, calcium and phosphorous would not be well absorbed and deficiencies of both could occur. But without cholesterol the whole process would not occur. Fats also help calcium enter our bones and muscles. Prostaglandins, made from fat, are responsible for this action. Other vitamins, including A, D, E, and K, rely on fat for proper absorption and utilization. These important vitamins are fat dependent for three reasons: First, they are most highly concentrated in fatty foods. Our bodies cannot produce a supply of these vitamins to assure our continued good health. Second, in order for these vitamins to be absorbed, there must be fat in the intestines. A low-fat diet may be deficient in these vitamins to begin with and might restrict their absorption. Third, once absorbed, these vitamins require lipoproteins, a combination of fat and protein, to carry them through the blood. Again, if there were no fat in the diet, these vitamins wouldn't get very far and wouldn't enhance our health.

My favorite function of fats is that they make food delightfully palatable. Let's face it, people love foods that contain fat, but they feel so guilty about eating them that they can't sit down at the dinner table and enjoy them. If properly balanced, fats will not be an unhealthy addition to your diet. And not only do they taste good but they make you feel good—psychologically as well as physiologically. Fats also satisfy physical hunger. People on low-fat diets often complain that they are always hungry. Well, of course they are: without fats in the diet they can't achieve a feeling of satiety. As a result, the brain just keeps sending the same message over and over: eat more, eat more. Because you never really feel satisfied, the temptation to overeat is irresistible. In fact, there's a good chance that you can actually gain weight on a low-fat diet by overeating to try and get that "I'm not hungry anymore" feeling. Besides, low-fat meals can be extremely unappetizing, often leading to an unbalanced diet. This problem is rampant in our geriatric population.

The Good, Bad, and Ugly Fats

Good fats include natural fats and oils, which contain important nutrients that our bodies cannot make, the *essential fatty acids.* These include the omega-6 and omega-3 oils found in nature. Here are some foods high in these good fats:

Vegetable Omega-6 Fats

Omega-6 fats are essential for good health and fitness. However, a diet too high in omega-6 fats may be a problem not only because of excess calories but because too high a level can cause metabolic imbalances similar to those found in persons who eat too much saturated or animal fat. Vegetable omega-6 fats are found in

- *most food oils: safflower, peanut, soy, sesame*
- *best supplement: black currant seed oil*
- *most vegetables (small amounts)*

Omega-3 Fats

Most people do not eat enough omega-3 fats.

- *beans, fish (salmon and sardines), most nuts and seeds, leafy vegetables (kale, Swiss chard, spinach, leaf lettuce)*
- *food oils: linseed (flax), walnut, pumpkin*
- *best supplements: EPA (fish oil), linseed (flax)*

Animal Fats

Some omega-6 fats are also found in animal fats (called *arachidonic acid*).

- *meat*
- *dairy*
- *egg yolks*
- *butter*
- *shellfish*

Most oils from vegetables are also called *polyunsaturated* (a chemical name), and many of those from animal fats are referred to as *saturated*. However, many fish contain polyunsaturated omega-3 fats, and many animal fats, such as egg yolks and beef, contain significant amounts of mono- or polyunsaturated fats. In addition, many vegetable oils such as coconut, palm, and peanut butter contain varying amounts of saturated fats.

Perhaps the best oil to use regularly is extra virgin olive oil. It's what makes the Mediterranean diet so healthy. Olive oil is mainly a *monounsaturated* fat and helps protect the body against heart disease, cancer, and other problems. Be sure to use only extra virgin olive oil; it's the highest grade (first pressed) and contains all the important nutrients, including antioxidants. Oils marked "pure" and "light" are far from it; they contain unwanted chemical solvents and are less nutritious.

Natural fats are not inherently bad, but if we don't balance them, they can turn bad. If you eat a balance of both types of omega fats, for example, you're doing well in terms of your balance of fat. But too many omega-6 fats may turn bad. When this happens, some of these good omega-6 fats can be converted to excess amounts of saturated fat, making them bad fats. This occurs more often if there's too much sugar in the diet. Bad fats cause too much inflammation in the body and increase your risk of heart disease and other conditions.

Beware of the ugly fats, as they are by far the most deadly. These are the artificial and chemically processed fats. They're usually listed on the labels of foods, and fortunately they're easy to spot. Unfortunately, however, they remain in the body for many weeks and months. Not only can they raise your cholesterol, but it's the bad LDL cholesterol that's elevated, while the good HDL cholesterol is reduced, increasing your risk for heart disease. Here are the ugliest fats:

- *Trans fats. These are found in hydrogenated and partially hydrogenated oils. Margarine is the most popular hydrogenated product.*

- *Heated oils. Most dangerous are the polyunsaturated oils. When heated, they produce chemicals called free radicals and are very unhealthy.*

- *Tropical oils. The most popular are palm and palm kernel oil.*

- *Fractionated oils. These are fats that are chemically processed to take out all the good omega oil, leaving only the saturated fat.*

By balancing your diet, you can greatly enhance the ability of the exercise component of your program to build an aerobic base, control stress, and burn more body fat.

BIBLIOGRAPHY

Textbooks

Maffetone, P., *Complementary Sports Medicine*. Champaign IL:
Human Kinetics, 1999.

McArdle, W. D., F. I. Katch, and V. L. Katch. *Exercise Physiology:
Energy, Nutrition, and Human Performance*. 3rd ed. Philadelphia:
Lea & Febiger, 1991.

Wilmore, J. H., and D. L. Costill. *Physiology of Sport and Exercise*.
Champaign IL: Human Kinetics, 1994.

Published Scientific and Medical Journal Papers

Abernathy, P., R. Thayer, and A. Taylor. "Acute and Chronic
Responses of Skeletal Muscle to Endurance and Sprint
Exercise." *Sports Medicine* 10, no. 6 (1990): 365–89.

Adlercreutz, H., M. Harkonen, K. Kuoppasalmi, H. Naveri,
I. Huhtaniemi, H. Tikkanen, K. Remes, A. Dessypris, and
J. Karvonen. "Effect of Training on Plasma Anabolic and
Catabolic Steroid Hormones and Their Response during
Physical Exercise." *International Journal of Sports Medicine* 7,
suppl. 1 (1986): 27–28.

Ahmaidi, S., P. Granier, Z. Taoutaou, J. Mercier, H. Dubouchaud,
and C. Prefaut. "Effects of Active Recovery on Plasma Lactate
and Anaerobic Power Following Repeated Intensive Exercise."
Medicine and Science in Sports and Exercise 28, no. 4 (1996):
450–56.

Aitken, J. C., and J. Thompson. "The Respiratory VCO_2/VO_2
Exchange Ratio during Maximum Exercise and Its Use As a
Predictor of Maximum Oxygen Uptake." *European Journal of
Applied Physiology and Occupational Physiology* 57, no. 6 (1988):
714–19.

————. "The Effects of Dietary Manipulation upon the Respiratory Exchange Ratio As a Predictor of Maximum Oxygen Uptake during Fixed Term Maximal Incremental Exercise in Man." *European Journal of Applied Physiology and Occupational Physiology* 58, no. 7 (1989): 722–27.

Amadio, P., Jr., D. M. Cummings, and P. Amadio. "Nonsteroidal Anti-inflammatory Drugs: Tailoring Therapy to Achieve Results and Avoid Toxicity." *Postgraduate Medicine* 93, no. 4 (1993): 73–76, 79–81, 85–88 passim.

Arena, B., N. Maffulli, F. Maffulli, and M. A. Morleo. "Reproductive Hormones and Menstrual Changes with Exercise in Female Athletes." *Sports Medicine* 19, no. 4 (1995): 278–87.

Bale, P., J. Doust, and D. Dawson. "Gymnasts, Distance Runners, Anorexics Body Composition and Menstrual Status." *Journal of Sports Medicine and Physical Fitness* 36, no. 1 (1996): 49–53.

Barrett, J., and T. Bilisko. "The Role of Shoes in the Prevention of Ankle Sprains." *Sports Medicine* 20, no. 4 (1995): 277–80.

Basmajian, J., and J. Bentzon. "An Electromyelographic Study of Certain Muscles of the Leg and Foot in the Standing Position." *Surgical and Gynecological Obstetrics* 98 (1954): 662–66.

Belanger, A., B. Candas, A. Dupont, L. Cusan, P. Diamond, J. L. Gomez, and F. Labrie. "Changes in Serum Concentrations of Conjugated and Unconjugated Steroids in 40- to 80-Year-Old Men." *Journal of Clinical Endocrinology and Metabolism* 79, no. 4 (1994): 1,086–90.

Bell, G. J., S. R. Petersen, J. Wessel, K. Bagnall, and H. A. Quinney. "Physiological Adaptations to Concurrent Endurance Training and Low Velocity Resistance Training." *International Journal of Sports Medicine* 12, no. 4 (1991): 384–90.

Bell, J. M., and E. J. Bassey. "Postexercise Heart Rates and Pulse Palpation As a Means of Determining Exercising Intensity in an Aerobic Dance Class." *British Journal of Sports Medicine* 30, no. 1 (1996): 48–52.

Bernton, E., D. Hoover, R. Galloway, and K. Popp. "Adaptation to Chronic Stress in Military Trainees: Adrenal Androgens, Testosterone, Glucocorticoids, IGF-1, and Immune Function." *Annals of the New York Academy of Sciences* 774 (1995): 217–31.

Bird, S. R., and S. Hay. "Pre-Exercise Food and Heart Rate during Submaximal Exercise." *British Journal of Sports Medicine* 21, no. 1 (1987): 27–28.

Bogdanis, G. C., M. E. Nevill, H. K. Lakomy, C. M. Graham, and G. Louis. "Effects of Active Recovery on Power Output during Repeated Maximal Sprint Cycling." *European Journal of Applied Physiology and Occupational Physiology* 74, no. 5 (1996): 461–69.

Boone, T., K. L. Frentz, and N. R. Boyd. "Carotid Palpation at Two Exercise Intensities." *Medicine and Science in Sports and Exercise* 17, no. 6 (1985): 705–9.

Boulay, M. R., J. A. Simoneau, G. Lortie, and C. Bouchard. "Monitoring High-Intensity Endurance Exercise with Heart Rate and Thresholds." *Medicine and Science in Sports and Exercise* 29, no. 1 (1997): 125–32.

Brandt, K. D. "Nonsteroidal Antiinflammatory Drugs and Articular Cartilage." *Journal of Rheumatology* 14, spec. no. (1987): 132–33.

Brizuela, G., S. Llana, R. Ferrandis, and A. C. Garcia-Belenguer. "The Influence of Basketball Shoes with Increased Ankle Support on Shock Attenuation and Performance in Running and Jumping." *Journal of Sports Sciences* 15, no. 5 (1997): 505–15.

Clanton, T. O., J. E. Butler, and A. Eggert. "Injuries to the Metatarsophalangeal Joints in Athletes." *Foot and Ankle* 7, no. 3 (1986): 162–76.

Clark, J. E., S. G. Scott, and M. Mingle. "Viscoelastic Shoe Insoles: Their Use in Aerobic Dancing." *Archives of Physical Medicine Rehabilitation* 70, no. 1 (1989): 37–40.

Cleak, M. J., and R. G. Eston. "Muscle Soreness, Swelling, Stiffness and Strength Loss after Intense Eccentric Exercise." *British Journal of Sports Medicine* 26, no. 4 (1992): 267–72.

Clyman, B. "Role of Non-Steroidal Anti-Inflammatory Drugs in Sports Medicine." *Sports Medicine* 3, no. 4 (1986): 342–46.

Colliander, E. B., G. A. Dudley, and P. A. Tesch. "Skeletal Muscle Fiber Type Composition and Performance during Repeated Bouts of Maximal, Concentric Contractions." *European Journal of Applied Physiology and Occupational Physiology* 58, nos. 1–2 (1988): 81–86.

Coyle, E. F., L. S. Sidossis, J. F. Horowitz, and J. D. Beltz. "Cycling Efficiency Is Related to the Percentage of Type I Muscle Fibers." *Medicine and Science in Sports and Exercise* 24, no. 7 (1992): 782–88.

Craig, B. W., J. Everhart, and R. Brown. "The Influence of High-Resistance Training on Glucose Tolerance in Young and Elderly

Subjects." *Mechanisms of Aging and Development* 49, no. 2 (1989): 147–57.

David, M. J., E. Vignon, M. J. Peschard, P. Broquet, P. Louisot, and M. Richard. "Effect of Non-Steroidal Anti-Inflammatory Drugs (NSAIDS) on Glycosyltransferase Activity from Human Osteoarthritic Cartilage." *British Journal of Rheumatology* 31, suppl. 1 (1992): 13–17.

Dieppe, P., J. Cushnaghan, M. K. Jasani, F. McCrae, and I. Watt. "A Two-Year Placebo-Controlled Trial of Non-Steroidal Anti-Inflammatory Therapy in Osteoarthritis of the Knee Joint." *British Journal of Rheumatology* 32, no. 7 (1993): 595–600.

Ding, J . H., C. B. Sheckter, B. L. Drinkwater, M. R. Soules, and W. J. Bremner. "High Serum Cortisol Levels in Exercise-Associated Amenorrhea." *Annals of Internal Medicine* 108, no. 4 (1988): 530–34.

Donnelly, A. E., R. J. Maughan, and P. H. Whiting. "Effects of Ibuprofen on Exercise-Induced Muscle Soreness and Indices of Muscle Damage." *British Journal of Sports Medicine* 24, no. 3 (1990): 191–95.

Dueck, C. A, K. S. Matt, M. M. Manore, and J. S. Skinner. "Treatment of Athletic Amenorrhea with a Diet and Training Intervention Program." *International Journal of Sport Nutrition* 6, no. 1 (1996): 24–40.

Duncan, B. B., L. E. Chambless, M. I. Schmidt, A. R. Folsom, M. Szklo, J. R. Crouse III, and M. A. Carpenter. "Association of the Waist-to-Hip Ratio Is Different with Wine Than with Beer or Hard Liquor Consumption." *American Journal of Epidemiology* 142, no. 10 (1995): 1,034–38.

Fisher, N. M., S. C. White, H. J. Yack, R. J. Smolinski, and D. R. Pendergast. "Muscle Function and Gait in Patients with Knee Osteoarthritis Before and After Muscle Rehabilitation." *Disability and Rehabilitation* 19, no. 2 (1997): 47–55.

Fry, A. C., and W. J. Kraemer. "Resistance Exercise Overtraining and Overreaching: Neuroendocrine Responses." *Sports Medicine* 23, no. 2 (1997): 106–29.

Gaesser, G. A., and L. A. Wilson. "Effects of Continuous and Interval Training on the Parameters of the Power-Endurance Time Relationship for High-Intensity Exercise." *International Journal of Sports Medicine* 9, no. 6 (1988): 417–21.

Gardner, L. I., Jr., J. E. Dziados, B. H. Jones, J. F. Brundage, J. M. Harris, R. Sullivan, and P. Gill. "Prevention of Lower Extremity Stress Fractures: A Controlled Trial of a Shock Absorbent Insole." *American Journal of Public Health* 78, no. 12 (1988): 1,563–67.

Goldberg, L., D. L. Elliot, and K. S. Kuehl. "Assessment of Exercise Intensity Formulas by Use of Ventilatory Threshold." *Chest* 94, no. 1 (1988): 95–98.

Grace, T. G., B. J. Skipper, J. C. Newberry, M. A. Nelson, E. R. Sweetser, and M. L. Rothman. "Prophylactic Knee Braces and Injury to the Lower Extremity." *Journal of Bone and Joint Surgery* 70, no. 3 (1988): 422–27.

Graves, J. E., A. D. Martin, L. A. Miltenberger, and M. L. Pollock. "Physiological Responses to Walking with Hand Weights, Wrist Weights, and Ankle Weights." *Medicine and Science in Sports and Exercise* 20, no. 3 (1988): 265–71.

Hakkinen, K., A. Pakarinen, M. Alen, H. Kauhanen, and P. V. Komi. "Neuromuscular and Hormonal Adaptations in Athletes to Strength Training in Two Years." *Journal of Applied Physiology* 65, no. 6 (1988): 2,406–12.

Hertel, J. "The Role of Nonsteroidal Anti-Inflammatory Drugs in the Treatment of Acute Soft Tissue Injuries." *Journal of Athletic Training* 32, no. 2 (1997): 350–58.

Hesse, S., D. Luecke, M. T. Jahnke, and K. H. Mauritz. "Gait Function in Spastic Hemiparetic Patients Walking Barefoot, with Firm Shoes, and with Ankle-Foot Orthosis." *International Journal of Rehabilitation Research* 19, no. 2 (1996): 133–41.

Hodgetts, V., S. W. Coppack, K. N. Frayn, and D. R. Hockaday. "Factors Controlling Fat Mobilization from Human Subcutaneous Adipose Tissue during Exercise." *Journal of Applied Physiology* 71, no. 2 (1991): 445–51.

Horne, L., G. Bell, B. Fisher, S. Warren, and A. Janowska-Wieczorek. "Interaction between Cortisol and Tumour Necrosis Factor with Concurrent Resistance and Endurance Training." *Clinical Journal of Sport Medicine* 7, no. 4 (1997): 247–51.

Horowitz, J. F., L. S. Sidossis, and E. F. Coyle. "High Efficiency of Type I Muscle Fibers Improves Performance." *International Journal of Sports Medicine* 15, no. 3 (1994): 152–57.

Hugenberg, S. T., K. D. Brandt, and C. A. Cole. "Effect of Sodium Salicylate, Aspirin, and Ibuprofen on Enzymes Required by the Chondrocyte for Synthesis of Chondroitin Sulfate." *Journal of Rheumatology* 20, no. 12 (1993): 2,128–33.

Iadarola, M. J., and R. M. Caudle. "Good Pain, Bad Pain." *Science* 278, no. 5336 (1997): 239–40.

Jones, B. H., D. N. Cowan, and J. J. Knapik. "Exercise, Training and Injuries." *Sports Medicine* 18, no. 3 (1994): 202–14.

Jones, B. H., D. N. Cowan, J. P. Tomlinson, J. R. Robinson, D. W. Polly, and P. N. Frykman. "Epidemiology of Injuries Associated with Physical Training among Young Men in the Army." *Medicine and Science in Sports and Exercise* 25, no. 2 (1993): 197–203.

Jorgensen, U. "Body Load in Heel-Strike Running: The Effect of a Firm Heel Counter." *American Journal of Sports Medicine* 18, no. 2 (1990): 177–81.

Karvonen, J., and T. Vuorimaa. "Heart Rate and Exercise Intensity during Sports Activities: Practical Application." *Sports Medicine* 5, no. 5 (1988): 303–11.

Keizer, H., G. M. Janssen, P. Menheere, and G. Kranenburg. "Changes in Basal Plasma Testosterone, Cortisol and Dehydro-epiandrosterone Sulfate in Previously Untrained Males and Females Preparing for a Marathon." *International Journal of Sports Medicine* 10, suppl. 3 (1989): S139–S145.

Kesavachandran, C., and S. Shashidhar. "Respiratory Function during Warm-up Exercise in Athletes." *Indian Journal of Physiology and Pharmacology* 41, no. 2 (1997): 159–63.

Khan, M. I. "Fracture Healing: Role of NSAIDs." *American Journal of Orthopedics* 26, no. 6 (1997): 413.

Kirwan, J. P., D. L. Costill, M. G. Flynn, J. B. Mitchell, W. J. Fink, P. D. Neufer, and J. A. Houmard. "Physiological Response to Successive Days of Intense Training in Competitive Swimmers." *Medicine and Science in Sports and Exercise* 20, no. 3 (1988): 255–59.

Krivickas, L. S. "Anatomical Factors Associated with Overuse Sports Injuries." *Sports Medicine* 24, no. 2 (1997): 132–46.

Kuipers, H. "Exercise-Induced Muscle Damage." *International Journal of Sports Medicine* 15, no. 3 (1994): 132–35.

Lambert, E. V., D. P. Speechly, S. C. Dennis, and T. D. Noakes. "Enhanced Endurance in Trained Cyclists during Moderate

Intensity Exercise Following Two Weeks Adaptation to a High Fat Diet." *European Journal of Applied Physiology* 69, no. 4 (1994): 287–93.

Leanderson, J., G. Nemeth, and E. Eriksson. "Ankle Injuries in Basketball Players." *Knee Surgery, Sports Traumatology, Arthroscopy* 1, nos. 3–4 (1993): 200–202.

Lehmann, M. J., W. Lormes, A. Opitz-Gress, J. M. Steinacker, N. Netzer, C. Foster, and U. Gastmann. "Training and Over-training: An Overview and Experimental Results in Endurance Sports." *Journal of Sports Medicine and Physical Fitness* 37, no. 1 (1997): 7–17.

Levine, B. D. "Regulation of Central Blood Volume and Cardiac Filling in Endurance Athletes: The Frank-Starling Mechanism as a Determinant of Orthostatic Tolerance." *Medicine and Science in Sports and Exercise* 25, no. 6 (1993): 727–32.

Maffetone, P. "A Hypothesis for the Clinical Evaluation of Aerobic and Anaerobic Function." *Sports Chiropractic Rehabilitation* 10, no. 2 (1996): 74–77.

McCarthy, J. P., J. C. Agre, B. K. Graf, M. A. Pozniak, and A. C. Vailas. "Compatibility of Adaptive Responses with Combining Strength and Endurance Training." *Medicine and Science in Sports and Exercise* 27, no. 3 (1995): 429–36.

McCarthy, J. P., M. M. Bamman, J. M. Yelle, A. D. Le Blanc, R. M. Rowe, M. C. Greenisen, S. M. Lee, E. R. Spector, and S. M. Fortney. "Resistance Exercise Training and the Orthostatic Response." *European Journal of Applied Physiology and Occupational Physiology* 76, no. 1 (1997): 32–40.

Miller, W. C., J. P. Wallace, and K. E. Eggert. "Predicting Max HR and the HR-VO_2 Relationship for Exercise Prescription in Obesity." *Medicine and Science in Sports and Exercise* 25, no. 9 (1993): 1,077–81.

Mills, P. C., N. C. Smith, I. Casas, P. Harris, R. C. Harris, and D. J. Marlin. "Effects of Exercise Intensity and Environmental Stress on Indices of Oxidative Stress and Iron Homeostatis during Exercise in the Horse." *European Journal of Applied Physiology and Occupational Physiology* 74, nos. 1–2 (1996): 60–66.

Moller, P., H. Wallin, and L. E. Knudsen. "Oxidative Stress Associated with Exercise, Psychological Stress and Life-Style Factors." *Chemico-Biological Interactions* 102, no. 1 (1996): 17–36.

Moore, A. D., Jr., S. M. Lee, M. C. Greenisen, and P. Bishop. "Validity of a Heart Rate Monitor during Work in the Laboratory and on the Space Shuttle." *American Industrial Hygiene Association Journal* 58, no. 4 (1997): 299–301.

Muoio, D. M., J. J. Leddy, P. J. Horvath, A. B. Awad, and D. R. Pendergast. "Effect of Dietary Fat on Metabolic Adjustments to Maximal VO₂ and Endurance in Runners." *Medicine and Science in Sports and Exercise* 26, no. 1 (1994): 81–88.

Murphy, P. J., and S. S. Campbell. "Nighttime Drop in Body Temperature: A Physiological Trigger for Sleep Onset?" *Sleep* 20, no. 7 (1997): 505–11.

Murphy, P. J., B. L. Myers, and P. Badia. "Nonsteroidal Anti-Inflammatory Drugs Alter Body Temperature and Suppress Melatonin in Humans." *Physiological Behavior* 59, no. 1 (1996): 133–39.

Nestler, J. E. "Assessment of Insulin Resistance." *Scientific American, Science and Medicine* September/October (1994): 58–67.

Newsholme, E. "Biochemical Mechanisms to Explain Immuno-suppression in Well-Trained and Overtrained Athletes." *International Journal of Sports Medicine* 15, suppl. 3 (1994): S142–S147.

Ng, A. V., R. Callister, D. G. Johnson, and D. R. Seals. "Endurance Exercise Training Is Associated with Elevated Basal Sympathetic Nerve Activity in Healthy Older Humans." *Journal of Applied Physiology* 77, no. 3 (1994): 1,366–74.

Nieman, D. C. "Immune Response to Heavy Exertion." *Journal of Applied Physiology* 82, no. 5 (1997): 1385–94.

Northover, B., B. P. O'Malley, and F. D. Rosenthal. "Alterations in Systolic Time Intervals in Primary Hypothyroidism as a Consequence of Warming." *Journal of Clinical Endocrinological Metabolism* 56, no. 1 (1983): 185–88.

O'Connor, P. J., W. P. Morgan, J. S. Raglin, C. M. Barksdale, and N. H. Kalin. "Mood State and Salivary Cortisol Levels Following Overtraining in Female Swimmers." *Psychoneuroendocrinology* 14, no. 4 (1989): 303–10.

Oldridge, N. B., W. L. Haskell, and P. Single. "Carotid Palpation, Coronary Heart Disease and Exercise Rehabilitation." *Medicine and Science in Sports and Exercise* 13, no. 1 (1981): 6–8.

Pedersen, B. K., T. Rohde, and M. Zacho. "Immunity in Athletes." *Journal of Sports Medicine and Physical Fitness* 36, no. 4 (1996): 236–45.

Pendergast, D. R., P. J. Horvath, J. J. Leddy, and J. T. Venkatraman. "The Role of Dietary Fat on Performance, Metabolism and Health." *American Journal of Sports Medicine* 24, suppl. 6 (1996): S53–S58.

Raven, P. B., and J. A. Pawelczyk. "Chronic Endurance Exercise Training: A Condition of Inadequate Blood Pressure Regulation and Reduced Tolerance to LBNP." *Medicine and Science in Sports and Exercise* 25, no. 6 (1993): 713–21.

Ring, C., and J. Brener. "Influence of Beliefs about Heart Rate and Actual Heart Rate on Heartbeat Counting." *Psychophysiology* 33, no. 5 (1996): 541–46.

Roberts, A. C., R. D. McClure, R. I. Weiner, and G. A. Brooks. "Overtraining Affects Male Reproductive Status." *Fertility and Sterility* 60, no. 4 (1993): 686–92.

Robbins, S. E., and A. M. Hanna. "Running-Related Injury Prevention through Barefoot Adaptations." *Medicine and Science in Sports and Exercise* 19, no. 2 (1987): 148–56.

Robbins, S., and E. Waked. "Balance and Vertical Impact in Sports: Role of Shoe Sole Materials." *Archives of Physical Medicine and Rehabilitation* 78, no. 5 (1997): 463–67.

———. "Hazard of Deceptive Advertising of Athletic Footwear." *British Journal of Sports Medicine* 31, no. 4 (1997): 299–303.

———. "Factors Associated with Ankle Injuries." *Sports Medicine* 25, no. 1 (1998): 63–72.

Robbins, S., E. Waked, G. J. Gouw, and J. McClaran. "Athletic Footwear Affects Balance in Men." *British Journal of Sports Medicine* 28, no. 2 (1994): 117–22.

Robbins, S., E. Waked, and J. McClaran. "Proprioception and Stability: Foot Position Awareness As a Function of Age and Footwear." *Age and Ageing* 24, no. 1 (1995): 67–72.

Robbins, S., E. Waked, and R. Rappel. "Ankle Taping Improves Proprioception Before and After Exercise in Young Men." *British Journal of Sports Medicine* 29, no. 4 (1995): 242–47.

Rosen, L. W., C. Smokler, D. Carrier, C. L. Shafer, and D. B. McKeag. "Seasonal Mood Disturbances in Collegiate Hockey Players." *Journal of Athletic Training* 31, no. 3 (1996): 225–28.

Rosenthal, N. E., D. A. Sack, J. C. Gillin, A. J. Lewy, F. K. Goodwin, Y. Davenport, P. S. Mueller, D. A. Newsome, and T. A. Wehr. "Seasonal Affective Disorder: A Description of the Syndrome and Preliminary Findings with Light Therapy." *Archives of General Psychiatry* 41, no. 1 (1984): 72–80.

Rovere, G. D., H. A. Haupt, and C. S. Yates. "Prophylactic Knee Bracing in College Football." *American Journal of Sports Medicine* 15, no. 2 (1987): 111–16.

Ruderman, N. B., S. H. Schneider, and P. Berchtold. "The 'Metabolically-Obese,' Normal-Weight Individual." *American Journal of Clinical Nutrition* 34, no. 8 (1981): 1,617–21.

Safran, M. R., W. E. Garrett Jr., A. V. Seaber, R. R. Glisson, and B. M. Ribbeck. "The Role of Warmup in Muscular Injury Prevention." *American Journal of Sports Medicine* 16, no. 2 (1988): 123–29.

Safran, M. R., A. V. Seaber, and W. E. Garrett Jr. "Warm-Up and Muscular Injury Prevention: An Update." *Sports Medicine* 8, no. 4 (1989): 239–49.

Sandvik, L., J. Erikssen, M. Ellestad, G. Erikssen, E. Thaulow, R. Mundal, and K. Rodahl. "Heart Rate Increase and Maximal Heart Rate during Exercise as Predictors of Cardiovascular Mortality: A Sixteen-Year Follow-Up Study of 1960 Healthy Men." *Coronary Artery Disease* 6, no. 8 (1995): 667–79.

Seaward, B. L., R. H. Sleamaker, T. McAuliffe, and J. F. Clapp III. "The Precision and Accuracy of a Portable Heart Rate Monitor." *Biomedical Instrumentation and Technology* 24, no. 1 (1990): 37–41.

Seidell, J. C., D. C. Muller, J. D. Sorkin, and R. Andres. "Fasting Respiratory Exchange Ratio and Resting Metabolic Rate as Predictors of Weight Gain: The Baltimore Longitudinal Study on Aging." *International Journal of Obesity-Related Metabolic Disorders* 16 (1992): 667–74.

Shepard, R. J., and P. N. Shek. "Impact of Physical Activity and Sport on the Immune System." *Reviews on Environmental Health* 11, no. 3 (1996): 133–47.

Simoneau, J. A., G. Lortie, M. R. Boulay, M. Marcotte, M. C. Thibault, and C. Bouchard. "Human Skeletal Muscle Fiber Type Alteration with High-Intensity Intermittent Training." *European Journal of Applied Physiology and Occupational Physiology* 54, no. 3 (1985): 250–53.

Sisto, S. A., J. LaManca, D. L. Cordero, M. T. Bergen, S. P. Ellis, S. Drastal, W. L. Boda, W. N. Tapp, and B. H. Natelson. "Metabolic and Cardiovascular Effects of a Progressive Exercise Test in Patients with Chronic Fatigue Syndrome." *American Journal of Medicine* 100, no. 6 (1996): 634–40.

Smith, L. L., M. H. Brunetz, T. C. Chenier, M. R. McCammon, J. A. Houmard, M. E. Franklin, and R. G. Israel. "The Effects of Static and Ballistic Stretching on Delayed Onset Muscle Soreness and Creatine Kinase." *Research Quarterly for Exercise and Sport* 64, no.1 (1993): 103–7.

Smith, R. L., G. Kajiyama, and N. E. Lane. "Nonsteroidal Anti-inflammatory Drugs: Effects on Normal and Interleukin 1 Treated Human Articular Chondrocyte Metabolism in Vitro." *Journal of Rheumatology* 22, no. 6 (1995): 1,130–37.

Snyder, A. C., H. Kuipers, B. Cheng, R. Servais, and E. Fransen. "Overtraining following Intensified Training with Normal Muscle Glycogen." *Medicine and Science in Sports and Exercise* 27, no. 7 (1995): 1,063–70.

Taha, A. S., W. Angerson, I. Nakshabendi, H. Beekman, C. Morran, R. D. Sturrock, and R. I. Russell. "Gastric and Duodenal Mucosal Blood Flow in Patients Receiving Non-Steroidal Anti-Inflammatory Drugs: Influence of Age, Smoking, Ulceration and Helicobacter pylori." *Alimentary Pharmacology and Therapeutics* 7, no. 1 (1993): 41–45.

Teitz, C. C., B. K. Hermanson, R. A. Kronmal, and P. H. Diehr. "Evaluation of the Use of Braces to Prevent Injury to the Knee in Collegiate Football Players." *Journal of Bone and Joint Surgery* 69, no. 1 (1987): 2–9.

Thonnard, J. L., D. Bragard, P. A. Willems, and L. Plaghki. "Stability of the Braced Ankle: A Biomechanical Investigation." *American Journal of Sports Medicine* 24, no. 3 (1996): 356–61.

Tomaro, J., and R. G. Burdett. "The Effects of Foot Orthotics on the EMG Activity of Selected Leg Muscles during Gait." *Journal of Orthopaedic Sports and Physical Therapy* 18, no. 4 (1993): 532–36.

Urhausen, A., H. Gabriel, and W. Kindermann. "Blood Hormones as Markers of Training Stress and Overtraining." *Sports Medicine* 20, no. 4 (1997): 251–76.

Vacek, L. "Incidence of Exercise-Induced Asthma in High School

Population in British Columbia." *Allergy and Asthma Proceedings* 18, no. 2 (1997): 89–91.

Van Mechelen, W., H. Hlobil, H. C. Kemper, W. J. Voorn, and H. R. de Jongh. "Prevention of Running Injuries by Warm-Up, Cool-Down, and Stretching Exercises." *American Journal of Sports Medicine* 21, no. 5 (1983): 711–19.

Whaley, M. H., L. A. Kaminsky, G. B. Dwyer, L. H. Getchell, and J. A. Norton. "Predictors of Over- and Underachievement of Age-Predicted Maximal Heart Rate." *Medicine and Science in Sports and Exercise* 24, no. 10 (1992): 1,173–79.

White, J. R. "EKG Changes Using Carotid Artery for Heart Rate Monitoring." *Medicine and Science in Sports and Exercise* 9 (1977): 88–94.

Wiesler, E. R., D. M. Hunter, D. F. Martin, W. W. Curl, and H. Hoen. "Ankle Flexibility and Injury Patterns in Dancers." *American Journal of Sports Medicine* 24, no. 6 (1996): 754–57.

Wright, V. "Historical Overview of Non-Steroidal Anti-Inflammatory Drugs." *British Journal of Rheumatology* 34, suppl. 1 (1995): 2–4.

INDEX

abdominal muscles, 151–52, 154

ab machines, 100. *See also* ski machines; stair and step machines; treadmills

acetaminophen, 137

active static stretching, 81. *See also* exercise; warm-ups

activity, 22–24

Addison's disease, 35

adrenal glands, 11, 85; and dietary fats, 175; functions of, 30; and low blood sugar, 34, 173; and overtraining, 87, 92; and stress, 29–30, 31–32, 142

adrenaline, 30

aerobic base, 48, 49, 92, 109–11, 147

aerobic deficiency syndrome (ADS), 82–86; and overtraining, 88, 89, 90, 92; questionnaire for, 4–5; signs of, 10–11

aerobic exercise: and anaerobic exercise, 37, 38, 52, 55, 87; benefits of, 22, 43, 47, 113; and blood pressure, 115; and bone strengthening, 42; and calorie burning, 44; and fat burning, 3, 7, 8, 22, 42, 43, 44, 47; and heart rate, 8, 59; and muscle bulk, 41–42; and stress reduction, 7; and sugar burning, 43; and warm-ups, 75. *See also* anaerobic exercise

aerobic system, 19–20; and antioxidant activity, 44, 49; contributions of, during activity, 50; and cooldown, 79; and endurance, 49; and fat burning, 20, 22, 49, 175; and hydration, 44; and injury, 49; measuring, 38; and muscle fibers, 20, 21; and recovery, 161; and walking, 91–92. *See also* anaerobic system

aging, 23; and aerobic exercise, 113; and bone loss, 115; nonfunctional years during, 83, 98; restoring youth, 112–17

Allen, Mark, 2

allergies: and adrenal dysfunction, 142; and stress, 33–34

amenorrhea, 11, 85, 90, 91

American Academy of Pediatrics, 98

American College of Sports Medicine, 39, 98

anaerobic exercise: and the abdominal muscles, 154; and aerobic exercise, 37, 38, 52, 55, 87; benefits of, 56; and blood pressure, 115; and calorie burning, 44; and cortisol, 38; and fat burning, 38, 39, 44; and free radicals, 44; and injury, 49, 136, 145–46, 149; interval training method of, 55–56; and the Maffetone Method, 8; and muscle bulking, 55; and overtraining, 91, 92, 145; problems caused by, 38–39; and recovery, 53, 79; rules for, 52–53, 55; and skipping rope, 100; and stress, 37–38; and sugar burning, 38; and treadmills, 100; and warm-ups, 75, 79; workouts for, 53–55. *See also* aerobic exercise

anaerobic system, 19, 22; contributions of, during activity, 50; development of, 51–56; and muscle fibers, 20–21; and sugar burning, 20–21. *See also* aerobic system

anemia, 44, 141

ankles, 128, 131, 132–33

antidepressants, 145. *See also* depression

antioxidant activity, in aerobic muscles, 22, 44, 49

anxiety, 11, 85. *See also* depression; stress

aspirin, 137

asthma, 33–34

atherosclerosis, 114. *See also* cholesterol, high

athletes: and dehydration, 44; and the Maffetone Method, 2; and MAF testing, 66; and overtraining, 162, 163, 164; and testosterone levels, 90

athletic shoes. *See* shoes

Ativan, 145

ballistic stretching, 81. *See also* exercise; warm-ups

barefoot, 127, 128, 129, 130, 133. *See also* jogging; running; shoes; walking

Basmajian, J., 129
Bentzon, J., 129
bicycling: and anaerobic exercise, 37, 51, 52; benefits of, 47; and bone strengthening, 42, 115; breathing for, 154; and fat burning, 3; and interval training, 56; and MAF testing, 68; and seasonal changes, 119–20; starting a program of, 99; stationary, 52, 99, 109
biking. *See* bicycling
blood sugar stress: and adrenal dysfunction, 173; and aerobic deficiency, 10, 84; and aerobic exercise, 115; and carbohydrates, 117, 173; and depression, 45
bone: loss of, 91, 115; strengthening, 42, 115. *See also* osteoporosis
Boston Marathon, 16
breast-feeding, 176. *See also* women
breathing, 20, 152–54. *See also* oxygen
bursitis, 139. *See also* injury; pain

calories, 44, 57, 178
cancer, 83, 98, 113, 170
carbohydrates: and body fat, 48, 84; cravings for, 125, 172; intolerance of, 3, 4–5, 10, 84, 167, 169–73; questionnaire for intolerance of, 4–5; and SAD, 125; test for intolerance of, 170–73; during training, 167,175; before workouts, 174–75
catacholamines, 30, 31
children, and exercise, 98–99
cholesterol, 2: benefits of, 176, 177; and carbohydrates, 170; and dietary fats, 180; and exercise rehabilitation, 112, 114, 116; and heart disease, 113; and stress testing, 39
cigarette smoking, 97, 113
circulation, poor, and aerobic deficiency, 11, 85–86
clothing, exercise, 123–24. *See also* shoes
colds, 31, 141, 142, 143
competition, 79–80; and carbohydrates, 174; less training for better performance in, 160, 161–62; and MAF testing, 73–74; and overtraining, 91; and recovery, 77, 79–80; and seasonal changes, 120–21; training schedules for, 160–65; and warm-ups, 79–80
cooling down, 77–79, 81, 149. *See also* exercise; warm-ups

cortisol: and anaerobic exercise, 38; and menstrual and menopausal problems, 11, 85; and overtraining, 89; and stress, 30, 31, 34
cross-country skiing, 3
cross training, 162, 164
cycling. *See* bicycling

dancing: as anaerobic exercise, 37, 51, 52; benefits of, 47; breathing during, 154; and fat burning, 3; and interval training, 56; starting an exercise program in, 99–100; and stretching, 80; and weights, 43
dehydration, 44, 124; and an aerobic base, 49; and MAF testing, 71; and NSAIDs, 137. *See also* water (drinking)
depression: and aerobic deficiency, 11, 85; and blood sugar, 45; and carbohydrate intolerance, 170, 173; and diet, 145; and the Maffetone Method, 2; and the neurotransmitters, 144–45; and overtraining, 90; and walking, 98. *See also* antidepressants; seasonal affective disorder (SAD)
DHEA, 30, 34; and menstrual and menopausal problems, 11, 85; and overtraining, 89, 90
diabetes, 2, 83; and aerobic exercise, 115; and carbohydrate intolerance, 170; and exercise rehabilitation, 112; and stress testing, 39; and walking, 98; and workout capability, 106. *See also* insulin
diaphragm, 151–52, 153, 154
diary, workout, 107–9, 111
diet, 7; and aerobic deficiency, 86; and aerobic exercise, 45; basic rules for, 166–69; and body fat, 50; and depression, 145; and injury, 74, 136, 144; and MAF test results, 66; and overtraining, 87; raw foods in, 168, 169; and stress, 27. *See also* carbohydrates; fat, dietary; obesity; protein; sugar; vitamins; weight gain
disease, aerobic exercise and, 44, 46
dizziness: cooling down to prevent, 78; and stress, 33
Dossey, Larry, 156, 157
dressing, for successful exercise, 123–24. *See also* shoes
duathletes, 162

Einstein, Albert, 155, 157, 158, 159
Elavil, 145. *See also* depression

electrolytes, 30, 31
endurance, 11, 25, 49, 85
epinephrine, 30, 31
equipment, exercise, 71–72, 107–9, 108, 109
essential fatty acids, 178
estrogen, 30; low, and bone loss, 34, 91. *See also* women; sex hormones
eustress, 28
exercise, 22–23, 24; to avoid, 100–101; and balance, 15–18; benefits of, 41–46, 116; best seasons for, 119–23; and children, 98–99; components of proper, 15–16; definition of, 24; dressing for, 123–24; and education, 26; and fun, 3; and increased activity, 23–24; as meditation, 24, 45, 92, 108–9; misconceptions about, xi, 41, 95–96, 100, 124, 162; "no pain, no gain" approach, xi, 2, 7, 26, 62, 106–7, 162; recommended, 97–100; and recovery, 2, 164; starting out, 95–103; and time, 155. *See also* cooling down; overtraining; warm-ups; workout program; *individual exercises*
exercise footwear. *See* shoes
exhaustion. *See* fatigue
eyes, sensitivity to light, and stress, 4, 33

fat, body, 2; and aerobic deficiency, 84; brown, 123, 124; and carbohydrate intolerance, 169; and heart rate, 2–3, 8; measuring, 9; and modifying your workout, 104; reasons for increased, 48; white, 123–24. *See also* obesity; weight gain
fat, dietary: to avoid, 167, 168, 174, 178–80; beneficial, 3, 175–79; and body fat, 84. *See also* carbohydrates; diet; obesity; protein; sugar; vitamins; weight gain
fat burning: and aerobic exercise, 3, 7, 8, 20, 44, 49; and anaerobic exercise, 44; and exercise clothing, 123–24; and insulin, 169; measuring, 21, 48–50; and snacking, 173–75; and sugar, 45
fatigue, 2; and adrenal stress, 142–43; and aerobic deficiency, 10, 84; and injury, 141, 143; and modifying your workout, 104; and overtraining, 88, 90; and stress, 3, 4, 33. *See also* depression; sleep dysfunction
feet. *See* barefoot; shoes
Fendler, Paul, 158

fitness, 18, 19; and health, 1, 7, 17–19
footwear. *See* shoes
fruits, 168–69

gas analyzer, 21, 48, 57
General Adaptation Syndrome (GAS), 32–33
glucocorticoids, 30, 31
goals, exercise, 6, 105–7

Hanna, A. M., 129
health: and fitness, 1, 7, 17–19; and fitness, questionnaire to evaluate, 4–5; and MAF testing, 71
heart disease, 2, 83; and carbohydrate intolerance, 170; and Eskimos, 176; and exercise, 113–14; and exercise rehabilitation, 112, 116; and inactivity, 97; and stress testing, 39; symptoms of, 39–40; and walking, 98; and workout capability, 106
heart monitors, 59, 64–65, 74; and exercise rehabilitation, 116; and starting an exercise program, 100; and warm-ups, 77; waterproof, 117
heart rate: and aerobic exercise, 8, 48; and body fat, 2–3, 8; and calorie burning, 57; and cooldown, 79; determining anaerobic or aerobic activity, 57–58; determining optimal, 59–63; and exercise, 57–58; measurement of, 58–63, 65 *(see also* heart monitors); and overtraining, 89
high blood pressure. *See* hypertension
hormones, 30, 31, 34. *See also* adrenal glands; *specific hormones*
hot tubs, 124
hunger, 141, 143. *See also* diet
hypertension, 2; 83, 112, 113, 116, 170; and aerobic exercise, 114–15; and carbohydrates, 117; and heart disease, 97; and stress testing, 39; and walking, 98

ibuprofen, 137
ilio-tibial band syndrome (ITB), 138, 147
illness, 61; oncoming, indications of, 72
immune system: and adrenal dysfunction, 142; and diet, 169; and excess stress, 31
infections, 31, 88, 141
inflammation, 30, 137, 140, 180. *See also* NSAIDs

injury, 104; and aerobic deficiency, 10, 84–85; and aerobic muscle fibers, 49; and anaerobic exercise, 38, 49, 51; ankle, 128, 131, 132; and arch function, 130–31, 132; causes of, 136, 138; chemical, 141–43, 146; functional, 147, 148; and imbalance, 19; joint, 10; mending, 146–50; mental or emotional, 143–46; and orthotics, 131–32; pathological, 147–48; prevention of, 74, 75; shoes as cause of, 8, 127, 128–30, 132, 135; and stretching, 80–81; structural, 138–40, 143, 146. *See also* "no pain, no gain"; pain

insomnia. *See* sleep dysfunction

insulin, 169, 173, 175, 177. *See also* diabetes

interval training, 55–56. *See also* anaerobic exercise; exercise; workout program

iron, 44–45

irritability, 141, 143

ITB. *See* ilio-tibial band syndrome

jet lag, 31

jogging: benefits of, 47; and bone strengthening, 42, 115; breathing during, 153–54; and seasonal changes, 119–20, 123. *See also* running; walking

Karvonen method, 61

lactation, 176

lactic acid, 38, 145–46. *See also* anxiety; depression; exercise; overtraining

Maffetone Method, 1–2, 6–9

Maffetone Method Questionnaire, 4–5

massage therapy, 147

maximum aerobic function (MAF), 47

Maximum Aerobic Function (MAF) test, 8, 48, 65, 66–69, 108, 111; and competition, 11, 73–74; factors affecting, 69–72; and overtraining, 88–89, 90; plateau in, 69

maximum aerobic heart rate, 61–63

meditation, 24, 36, 45, 92, 108–9, 156

men: and body fat, 9, 50; and bone loss, 91, 115; hormonal factors in, effect on MAF test, 70; and reaction times, 113. *See also* testosterone

menopausal problems, and aerobic deficiency, 11, 85. *See also* women

menstrual problems: and aerobic deficiency, 11, 85; and overtraining, 90–91. *See also* women

mineralcorticoids, 30, 31

Mittleman, Stu, 2

Moller, Lorraine, 2, 156, 157

muscles: aerobic, benefits of building, 19–22, 41–42, 44, 45, 47, 49; anaerobic, and training, 38, 55, 56; bulky, avoiding, 41–42; and cooldown, 78, 149; endurance, providing, 49; fat and sugar burning in, 20, 21, 22, 48–49; and hormones, 30, 31, 90; injury, resistance to, 49, 75; and lactic acid, 38, 145–46; and NSAIDS, 137; and shoes, 129–30, 133; stress on, 119, 139; stretching, 80–81, 149; support for weak, 131–32; and walking, 97; and warm-ups, 75, 76, 77, 149. *See also* abdominal muscles; aerobic exercise; anaerobic exercise; diaphragm; exercise

musculoskeletal symptoms: and aerobic deficiency, 84–85; and stress, 34

neurotransmitters, 144, 145. *See also* depression

New York City Marathon, 16–17

"no pain, no gain," xi, 2, 7, 26, 61, 62, 106–7, 162

norepinephrine, 30, 31, 144, 145

NSAIDs (nonsteroidal anti-inflammatory drugs), 137, 139

nutrition. *See* diet

obesity, 2; and aerobic deficiency, 10; and aerobic exercise, 113; and exercise rehabilitation, 112; measuring, 9; and stress testing, 39. *See also* diet; fat, body; weight gain

obsession, 28. *See also* overtraining

oligomenorrhea, 90–91

omega-3 fats, 176, 178, 179

omega-6 fats, 178–79, 179–80

180-Formula, 59–60, 61–63, 116

orthotics, 131–32

osteoporosis: and aging, 115; and amenorrhea, 91; and exercise rehabilitation, 112; and walking, 98, 117. *See also* bone

overreaching, 89

overtraining, 25–26, 87, 99; and adrenal dysfunction, 87, 89; and aerobic exercise, 49; and anaerobic exercise, 39, 51; by athletes, 162, 163, 164; correction of, 66, 91–92; and dis-

ordered eating, 91; and heart rate, 60;
and injury, 26, 144, 145, 147; and
insufficient recovery, 24; and obsession, 28; prevention of, 74; and seasonal changes, 120; stages of, 88–90,
92; and stress, 34, 87, 121, 145;
symptoms of, 88
overweight. *See* obesity; weight gain
oxygen: and definition of aerobic, 20;
gas analyzer used to measure consumption of, 21, 60; VO_2max, 60–61

pain, 5, 8, 32, 33, 40, 105, 148, 149;
avoiding, 1, 26, 102, 138–40, 150. *See
also* injury; "no pain, no gain"
parasympathetic overtraining, 90. *See
also* overtraining
passive recovery, 77
passive stretching, 81. *See also* exercise; warm-ups
phospholipids, 175
physical therapy, 147
Pigg, Mike, 2
potassium, 30
pregnancy, 176. *See also* children;
women
progesterone, 30; low, and bone loss,
91. *See also* women; sex hormones
prostaglandins, 175, 177
protein, 172, 173, 177
Prozac, 145. *See also* depression

questionnaire, 4–5

range of motion: and stretching, 80,
81; and taping joints, 131; warm-ups
improving, 77
recovery, 24; and the aerobic system,
161; and anaerobic exercise, 53, 79;
in competition, 77, 79–80, 164
rehabilitation, 112–18, 155
Reye's Syndrome, 137
Robbins, S., 129
rope skipping, 100
rowing: and anaerobic exercise, 51, 52,
101; and fat burning, 3; and interval
training, 56
runner's knee, 138
running, 96; and anaerobic exercise,
51, 52; and bone strengthening, 42,
115; breathing during, 153–54; and
fat burning, 3; and injury, 129, 138;
and seasonal changes, 119–20; shoes
for, 43, 135; and time, 155; and
weights, 43. *See also* jogging; walking

salt, 167, 168
saunas, 124
scoliosis, 91
seasonal affective disorder (SAD), 118,
125–26; and adrenal dysfunction,
125; and stress, 29, 35; symptoms of,
125; treatment of, 125–26. *See also*
depression
seasons, adapting to, 118–26. *See also*
weather
Selye, Hans, 31–32
serotonin, 144–45. *See also* depression
sex drive, diminished: and aerobic deficiency, 11, 86; and SAD, 125; and
stress, 3, 11, 34, 86
sex hormones, 30, 31, 34. *See also specific hormones*
shoes, 42–43, 102; and arch function,
130–31; injuries caused by, 1, 8, 127,
128–30, 132, 133, 135, 139, 140, 150;
and MAF testing, 71; misconceptions about, 127, 128; purchasing,
43, 132–33, 134; versus going barefoot, 127, 128, 129, 130, 133
short leg, 140
skating, 3
skiing, cross-country, 3
ski machines, 101. *See also* ab
machines; stair and step machines;
treadmills
skipping rope, 100
sleep dysfunction: and aerobic deficiency, 11, 85; and injury, 141; and
SAD, 125; and stress, 3, 4, 29, 33, 34,
142–43
smoking, 97, 113
Snider's Test, 153, 154
sodium, 30
Space, Time, and Medicine (Dossey),
156, 157
"spot" reducing, 84, 100
stair and step machines: and anaerobic
exercise, 52; and beginning an exercise program, 101; benefits of, 47;
and bone strengthening, 42; breathing while using, 154; and interval
training, 56. *See also* ab machines; ski
machines; treadmills
static stretching, 81
steam rooms, 124
straw exercise, to train diaphragm
muscle, 153
stress, 28; and the adrenal glands,
29–30, 83, 142; and aerobic deficiency, 11, 85; and the aerobic system, 110; and the anaerobic system,